Christopher Schaefer
Tijno Voors

VISION
IN ACTION

The Art of Taking and Shaping Initiatives

GW00702005

HAWTHORN PRESS
ANTHROPOSOPHIC PRESS

More and more of us are now moving out of conventional full-time employment, some voluntarily, others through no choice of our own. As this trend continues, there is a growing need for advice and guidance on new ways of working.

How do we start, how do we finance, and how do we manage new initiatives like community farms, community schools, local employment projects, local wholefood co-operatives? These differ in institutional form, ethical outlook and corporate objectives from conventional organisations in the private and public sectors. Conventional practitioners of accounting, finance, company law, business management and public administration often can't help us.

I welcome *Vision in Action* for the insights it brings to these questions and the answers to them. I am sure that many readers, not only in the voluntary and 'alternative' sectors, will find it a valuable source of inspiration and help.

James Robertson

Schaefer, Christopher – Voors, Tijno
Vision in action : the art of taking and shaping initiatives. – (Social Ecology series; v.4)
1. Community development
I. Title II. Voors, Tijno III. Series 307'.14 HN49.C6

ISBN 0-9507062-9-9

ISBN 0 950 7062 9 9

Vision in Action is published by Hawthorn Press, The Mount, Whiteshill, Stroud GL6 6JA in the United Kingdom. It is published by Anthroposophic Press, Bells Pond, Star Route, Hudson, New York 12534, in the U.S.A.

Typeset in Baskerville by Q-Set, 2 Conway Road, Hucclecote, Gloucester GL3 3PL, U.K.

Printed by Billings & Son Ltd., Hylton Road, Worcester, U.K.

Dedication

This book is dedicated to Bons and Signe who have tolerated, encouraged and suffered the vagaries of our travelling work life.

Acknowledgements

Grateful acknowledgements for help with publishing this book are made to the Mercury Provident Society Ltd., Marcus Wulfling, the Centre for Social Development for permission to reproduce some exercises, Hugh Barton, Ross Jennings, George Perry and Malcolm Leary.

Contents

Introduction

Christopher Schaefer

As individuals we are confronted with a host of societal issues over which we appear to have little control. The complexity of the questions, the size of governmental bureaucracies, the untransparency of the political process and the weight of everyday concerns combine to breed a feeling of powerlessness. Yet there is an area in which we can and do make a difference – the realm of initiative, of social creation. In the development of shops, educational centres, service institutions, volunteer programmes, small companies and in the transformation of human relationships our ideas and our acts do matter. The social world is a humanly created world. How an office looks, the quality of a product, and the manner in which co-workers talk to each other can be shaped and altered by our deeds.

This book is about the social creation process and is for initiative-takers, in fact for all of us to the degree that we consciously choose to affect the social environment we live and work in. It is of particular relevance for individuals and groups who are starting or have started schools, shops, community projects, therapeutic centres or small businesses and want to work on a co-operative basis. What it offers are principles, perspectives and guidelines to widen the realm of choice and to encourage the will for taking initiatives which serve the spirit, the human being and the earth.

Much of the content of this book was developed in a course on community development given at the Centre for Social Development, Emerson College, England. It also draws on our experiences as consultants and facilitators with a wide variety of small and medium sized clients in England, Holland and the United States. For many of our basic concepts we are indebted to our colleagues in the member institutions of the NPI Association for Social Development.[1]

The philosophical and spiritual orientation brought to the subject is based on the work of Rudolf Steiner, the Austrian philosopher and educator who was the founder of Anthroposophy and of Waldorf education, as well as contributing to a process of renewal in a variety of other disciplines. However, the book is meant for the general reader and presupposes no special knowledge or vocabulary other than an interest in social questions.

To encourage the taking of initiatives and the exploration of the ideas contained in this book I cannot think of more sage advice that that given by Goethe:

> 'Concerning all acts of initiative and creation there is one elementary truth the ignorance of which kills countless ideas and splendid plans; that the moment one definitely commits oneself, then Providence moves too. All sorts of things occur to help one that would otherwise not have occurred. A whole stream of events issues from the decision raising in one's favour all manner of unforeseen incidents and meetings and material assistance which no man could have dreamed would have come his way. Whatever you can do, or dream you can do, do it. Boldness has genius, power and magic in it. Begin it now.'

Advent 1985 – Spring Valley, New York

Chapter One

Starting and Nurturing Initiatives

Tijno Voors

How can we foster the development of initiatives? How can new enterprises such as community projects, schools, farms and businesses be well founded? How can we work together as equals, sharing our responsibilities, encouraging each other in our development, and offering a high quality product or service?

These are questions many people ask. They are searching and experimenting to find ways to take and sustain new initiatives that make a contribution to social renewal.

Many projects begin with great enthusiasm, good intentions, useful ideas, capable people and the necessary resources. But many of these initiatives never really start, or disappear after a short period. Other initiatives evolve, become visible, active and successful, but are soon entangled in all kinds of difficulties and conflicts.

Undertaking an initiative with others means working long hours every day, many meetings, having a small income, taking great risks, tiredness, lack of rhythm, and the feeling of never being able to realise the ideal. It also means sharing responsibility and possibilities to experiment and learn. And sometimes it means realising ideals and sharing great successes.

In all my contacts with new initiatives over the last ten years I have been confronted time and again with the question: How can we make our initiative *work*? In reviewing their history, I often noticed that some aspects were neglected and others over-emphasised. The key for a more systematic approach and review of initiatives was finally provided when Ronnie Lessem, while working with URBED, introduced me to the concept of *'From Vision to Action'* developed by Kevin Kingsland.[1] This concept helped me realise that every initiative needs to nurture *seven basic aspects*. These are:-

  – Developing vision – recognising the motive
  – Answering a need
  – Formulating direction
  – Commitment of people
  – Working together
  – Managing processes and time
  – Finding facilities and resources.

When starting up, all initiatives go through a process of birth involving the seven basic aspects.

There is an idea and a need is seen. Brochures are made indicating the direction. A group that is really committed to work is looked for and the initiative can start only if it can find a building, finances, and can organise its work activities and its way of working together. In this process, some aspects receive a lot of attention and are discussed and wrestled with at length, while others are only mentioned at the beginning but not recognised as important and so will have to be dealt with later on.

In the following pages I want to describe the nature of the seven basic aspects.

1. Developing Vision – Recognising the Motive

Sometimes we meet someone who has lived for a long time with an idea to start something – be it a new approach to existing work, a new centre, a workshop, a café, a business, a school, a new institute or agency. They have been carrying around the germ of the idea – it keeps coming back to them time and time again as a picture of what might be. Like a dream. But circumstances somehow contrive to never allow it to happen.

Then all of a sudden they meet some person who looks as if they too have been waiting for the same thing to happen. Then they may meet another.....and another.....who has a friend who.....! Maybe the only thing they have in common is the idea. They begin to share their dreams, talk to each other with great enthusiasm, become excited and start making all kinds of tentative plans. Sometimes they may get a little carried away – but never mind! It is as if inside each one of them something significant has been touched. This something wants to get out, begin moving, start to happen.

This is the source of the vision – a picture, image of that which lives in the will of each initiative taker. In every initiative there is a need to make this explicit, as clear as possible – and to share it. This can be difficult to do, for the stirrings inside are not easy to put into words, to capture enough to relate to others. If we wait awhile and listen hard one of the initiative takers may be able to make a start, to put their feelings into words, helping others who cannot formulate these feelings so exactly.

When you want to take an initiative with a group of people who equally share the responsibility for the whole, then it is of utmost importance to develop *a sense of the motives which live in the different initiative takers*. People bring their life experiences, their values, their expectations to the initiative and everyone's life brings different colours. In their first enthusiasm they tend to see only that they agreed and do not notice their differences. But later when there is no time, when there is pressure, the differences are felt and can be the source of conflicts.

So it is worthwhile at the start and also regularly in later years to find time to sit together and to listen to each person's individual goals and recognise the common goals. I sometimes ask: 'If this were an enterprise where you could realise your ideals, your hopes, your expectations, which would be the most important to realise?' If you then listen to these highly individual stories, the whole group can get a feeling of what there is in common and what differences have to be accommodated.

Through questions to each other, people start to realise that working together in a group brings much more than just skills. Everyone brings something that lives deeply hidden in his or her soul. Deep in their hearts, every person is searching for their life path, to meet their destiny. And in the process of meeting and working with others, something of one's destiny can be realised, something which one cannot realise alone.

Interest in the individuality of the other and respect for what is different are the basic attitudes which must exist in a group of people if it wants to create something together. Self-interest and the over-valuing of one's own vision will in the long run create tensions and conflicts. People in an initiative can regularly ask each other:

- What do *you* want to realise in this initiative? Why is that important to us? What ideals, hopes, expectations can be realised? What guiding principles do you want to realise?
- What changes would this bring to our lives? How does this step relate to the rest of my biography?

And listening to the contributions one can ask:

- What do we have in common and what differences do we have to accommodate?

There is still another aspect to the recognition of the motive.

When a group of people work together the individuals in the group can achieve something together that cannot be achieved by each person alone. Just as with human beings – an initiative has an identity, something that makes it unique. A hundred schools may follow the same curriculum, but none of them is the same. So we must ask ourselves, what makes one school different from the other? Is it the alchemy of the different people or is it something of a higher nature that wants to find expression through people?

So people in initiatives can sometimes ask themselves or others:

- What is the identity of our work?
- What is it that wants to live between us?
- What can we make possible together?

2. Answering a Need

Initiatives that want to respond to the social or economic questions of today cannot only spring from an inner urge to do something. They must also be directed towards what other people are asking. The aim of every organisation is *to meet the needs of others;* to respond to the questions and demands of their customers, clients, pupils, parents.

But how do you find out what people want, expect and need?

An interesting approach to this question has been developed by Forum 3, a life centre in Stuttgart, West Germany. The life centre is in the centre of the city, where people meet every evening in a coffee house or come together in study or action groups; they do artistic activities, or discuss contemporary political, social or economic questions. Twice a year, staff members of Forum 3 invite their 'customers' to look behind the scene of the activities of Forum 3 and indicate what they appreciate.

'Customers' are asked: what they expect, and what they

would like offered as activities. The Forum staff listens and asks. Later they review and conclude which activities need to be changed, developed, or discontinued. In this way, the staff tries to keep and develop a living contact with the larger group and serves what is really wanted. Once a year, the staff members of Forum 3 do something else in a similar direction. They ask themselves what questions that concern them are gradually surfacing. Through this process, they try to recognise signs of the times, and as a result they are often able to anticipate and prepare themselves for the demands of two or three years later.

The key to finding out what is asked, demanded, or needed is to try to creep into the skin of the customers. Members of the initiative group must be open to every suggestion – look at it, taste it, weigh it. As someone once said to me: 'Every suggestion by someone is a starting point for further thinking about the chances and reality of our initiative.' The danger with everything you want to offer is that you are too self-confident and believe you know what is the best. On the other hand, do not lose your sense of direction by following every hint, or doubting with every critical note.

To know what is wanted, to meet the interest of customers, an initiative must become visible. Members of the group will have to go out and speak about the initiative and see how people respond. To get information they have to be alert and observe well; they have to listen. At the start they may speak with friends, visit similar initiatives in other places or countries, organise evenings, meet with local politicians, write articles, listen to the responses, and see if they can find support.

Supporters are very important for an initiative that wants to stand in the world. True supporters are invaluable with their concrete suggestions, their help with the work, their smaller or larger financial backing, their warmth, interest, and support – especially in the early days. Very few initiatives have come to birth without the help and sacrifice of many invisible wives, husbands, children, friends, volunteers. Supporters are the warmth body of an initiative, they are the 'mother' of the initiative; they prepare the environment.

Experiences with initiatives that are looking for financial support have also shown that it is helpful to find a number of supporters and ask them for a personal loan, or to act as a personal guarantor for a loan. (See Chapter Five).

It is essential to stay in touch with the customers, to know what they want in the later years of an organisation. You can wait for parents to send their children to another school, or anticipate the changes that will prepare pupils to meet the challenges of the Eighties and Nineties. If every organisation would ask itself every year if it were still responding to the needs of its customers, fewer would be in trouble.

Asking the following questions will help you identify the needs of the people served by the initiative:

- Are we listening, observing, asking our customers what they expect of us?
- What do people really express in their needs? How do we know that the initiative is wanted?
- What needs, expectations, do people express that could be incorporated in the initiative or even give it a change of emphasis?
- What opportunities and what restrictions lie in the situation one meets?
- Are people willing and able to pay a price for our services?
- What are the current questions facing us, and what response are we making?

Of course you can never be totally sure the needs have been met until your customers have bought the product, or filled the school.

3. Formulating Direction

At a certain moment the initiative has to become more specific. It is good to have a dream, a great vision, or a deep motive to contribute something that brings social renewal. But these are often very large gestures which will be realised only in the distant future. It is necessary to confront this vision with the needs, the possibilities, and the limitations that are becoming visible.

Members of the initiative have to develop a picture of how the initiative will function in two or three years' time. The time has come to stop orientating themselves by asking others what they expect and listening to their suggestions. It is time to become concrete. An excellent instrument for this is to start writing a brochure or to prepare material for a fund-raising appeal. In doing so, you dive into the process of formulating and reformulating, and have to guard against becoming abstract. What is written has to interest people, has to make them stop for a moment, has to work on their imagination.

You need a lot of imagination here in order to develop a living picture of the future. You have to play with words, but also with forms, colours, so that gradually an image of the school, the business, the curative home, or the counselling service becomes visible.

A brochure has to express:

- The name of the initiative or the product.
- Artistic representations of a central aspect of the name or the activities of the initiative.
- A short description of the history, the motive and the general aims.
- A description of what members want to have achieved in the next two or three years i.e. what activities will be developed.
- A description of the basic attitude, style, approach to customers, co-workers, finances and organisation.

Formulating the direction is a confronting, painful, and sometimes agonising process. One or two people will write; but will the product express what lives in the others? Often things are expressed that have not been discussed at all, and pressure builds up to agree because the appeal must go out. There the first cracks in the beautiful harmony will start to show.

This process of choosing and formulating the direction is a constant recurring necessity. New developments take place, the initiative grows, new products, services, classes, courses are offered. In many initiatives the move to a new building is a milestone in the biography of the initiative. You have to build or renovate. And again, you have to formulate, to choose direction.

For example, a school approached parents, friends, supporters with an extensive brochure appealing to build 'OUR SCHOOL', and inviting parents and others to express very concretely which building skills, materials, tools, could be made available.

All this is not only meant to reveal to the public what members of the initiative see as the central aims, style, and activities of the organisation. It can also serve as a focal point for discussions between the co-workers. Everyone should ask him or herself if they share this living picture of the future.

Exercise: Formulating Direction

Making a Poster or Advertisement

A good exercise to work on the common direction of the initiative is to spend an evening with co-workers, making a poster or an advertisement for a special event, or a title page for a course brochure, or an appeal leaflet.

1. Someone describes in short the main aspects of the event or coming activity.

2. Every co-worker makes a poster, advertisement or title page using words, key sentences, pictures, logo, lay-out, colours.

3. Co-workers share their work and a discussion follows on which words, sentences, pictures and colours would draw attention and interest to the event.
   One can also discuss whether the poster expresses the true nature of the initiative.

4. Commitment of People

The three above-mentioned aspects of recognising the motive, answering a need, and formulating direction, will bring the underlying values of the initiative into consciousness. This process of becoming conscious of what people share and want to bring to expression together is very important for people of today. Many more people want to contribute concretely by sharing the responsibility instead of following the leader, the boss, the director. However, people can start to act intelligently in the sense of the whole, only if the direction, the vision of the future gradually becomes explicit. So initiatives that want to further co-responsibility have to return to these stages time and again in order to rekindle the flame that fired them. This process is also necessary for new people who join the initiative later, to give them an opportunity to connect with the aims.

There is, however, a danger of talking too much, of trying to bring everything to consciousness, of waiting until everyone has said that they will support the initiative. Potential co-workers, but also supporters and volunteers get impatient and want to see something starting to happen. You have to start moving – someone must be willing to give up his previous job; another must follow; real preparation for action has to start. You will often see that the initiative group changes significantly. People have to take a step, risk their jobs, their income, the well-being of their family, without the certainty of success and security. This seems less of a problem in the Eighties where so many people are already out of work. But it still remains an enormous step in which you not only commit yourself but also the people who are dependent on you.

I remember a group of people who had been meeting together to prepare an initiative for working with young people. They were people with very different backgrounds: a gardener, a printer, a management consultant, a social worker, a maintenance man, a lecturer, an artist. When the step to begin was taken there were only two who could commit themselves; the others moved to the periphery, became supporters, volunteers who were closely associated. After a year most of them had moved and were involved in other things. At the same time, other people came forward, free to get going. Sometimes it looks as if some smoke signals have gone through the valleys and over the hills, because people from far and wide have heard and want to join.

The process of starting confronts the initiative takers with the ever-returning question: *'How do we find our real partners?'*. People who want to join have all kinds of different motives; how do you find the criteria to choose among them? You are confronted here with one of the hardest questions of life. People's feet have brought them to this place. Are they passing by, are they asking for shelter, are they bringing the skills needed to offer quality, are they fitting into the team? You cannot be sure in the first meeting but have to guard against hurried commitments. Especially when finding your colleagues you have to take time. I know of a school that is in great need of some teachers. People come to fill the job, but when the personnel group of the school, and especially one person who is respected for her clear, deep and mostly sound judgement, express reservations, then the person is not invited to join and the children do not have that subject. This example stands in strong contrast to the attitude of another school that invited people to join as teachers because the children needed a teacher. The result of that policy is that this school has too many colleagues who do not understand the basic direction of the school.

A way of approaching this question is to make it a policy to answer the following questions:

1. Do we see each other as *initiative* partners, carriers of the same aims and impulse, wanting to serve similar needs?
2. Are we willing to share a *destiny* together respecting each other in the differences and accepting the consequences of each other's activities?
3. Do we have the capacities that are needed *to do the work* and are our capacities and skills complementing each other?

In other words, are we meeting our initiative, destiny and work-partners? You can say this also in a very different way as was done to develop a personnel policy for a company that

makes natural medicine. They try to approach every vacancy filled from inside or outside, by asking themselves the following questions:
Is the person:

- Willing and capable of doing the job?
- Willing and capable of working together with us?
- Caring for the aims and development of the Company?
- Willing to accept the salary policy?

The last point came in to emphasise the different character of the salary arrangements in this Company.

These questions can never be answered with a straight yes or no, but answers will emerge in conversations and working together.

To find out if there is a group that is really willing to commit itself to the work, the following questions might be helpful:

- What risks are people willing and able to take?
- Is there enough patience, endurance, courage and commitment in the group to succeed?
- Who are the carriers, who are the supporters, the volunteers?
- What personal investment of others (dependants) or resources of others are we risking with this step?

5. *Working Together*

Every group that has decided to work together to answer an identified need has to start to organise itself. Every small or large initiative has to nurture a whole network of relationships.

When we look more closely at these relationships we can

distinguish among them by the degree of direct involvement in the enterprise.

First of all you have the group that consists of customers (e.g. clients, patients or parents), suppliers, banks, local and government institutions, and so on. The initiative can aim to develop a regular contact with groups of customers. It is becoming more and more important to connect with similar initiatives or enterprises in the region, thus forming an association or network as a source for professional exchange.[2] Many of these associations or networks exist among schools, curative homes, shops and consultants. They often provide a platform for the exchange and development of ideas about new approaches, methods and concepts.

These associations or networks, in which every institution stays independent, work on the basis of recognised interdependence and trust, and the understanding is that by complementing and supporting every one, each group has more chance of a mature organisation. A circle of relations closer to the initiative is made of the supporters, volunteers, guarantors, financial benefactors, accountant or bookkeepers, and of course the trustees or members of the Board.

These people often play a very important role during the starting period of initiatives. Not so much because they have a formal position on the Board, but because they strengthen the initiative with their expertise, guidance, extra donations, enthusiasm, or unlimited supply of helping hands. Their role can sometimes be influential, as was the case with a school where a group of parents made all the plans and organised all the finances for the development of the school and a move to a new building. The parent group sent their plans to the teachers, but moved it further when the teachers did not respond in two or three weeks. The parents were actually more worried about their unbalanced relationship than the teachers. In more established schools, one usually sees the reverse. The teachers decide everything and use the parents when it suits them.

This circle of real supporters is of vital importance for the life of every organisation. It is the warmth body without which no institution can stay healthy in the long run. Their honesty, concern, wisdom and respect can keep the co-workers awake, alert and open to new developments. The supporters provide the fresh air in which the initiative can breathe.

The closest circle of relationships that has to be nurtured is the group of co-workers. How do they work together? How do they make decisions? How do they organise the work responsibilities? How do they deal with salaries, ownership and profit-sharing? These questions are born out of a longing to find new social forms that are challenging, that open the possibility to take responsibility, to learn to develop. These forms are not more efficient or easier; they do not create more harmonious relationships. They challenge, and demand of people a new social understanding, an attitude of interest and respect in the others, and the use of social skills. Especially when working together to build co-responsibility you meet each other and yourself more intensely. It is my experience that no new social forms succeed without the commitment of the co-workers to work on themselves. (See Chapter Six).

One often sees that when there are strong expectations and verbal acknowledgements to work together as equals, the reality may be very different. Then the initiative begins to struggle with crises after a while, giving rise to all kinds of misunderstandings, bad feelings, heated arguments and, ultimately, conflict.

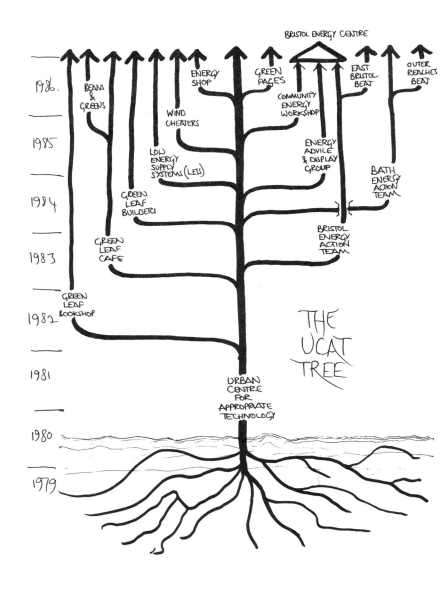

Family Tree of Initiatives
Fostered by the Urban Centre for Appropriate Technology in
Bristol

RELATIONSHIP MAP

Working together needs to take place on several levels around the organisation. Co-workers, supporters, and clients are all involved in various dialogues. Association is based upon freely willed dialogue. It cannot be legislated, but is created out of the recognition that each independent unit can be strengthened in such a relationship.

Co-Workers
How do we make decisions?
How do we deal with salaries?

Ownership? Profit Sharing? etc.Focus is on internal arrangements.

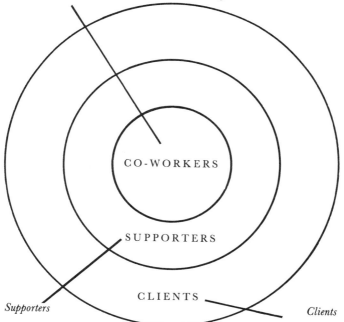

Supporters

Become Board members, formalizing the initial warmth and enthusiasm. Forms arise – legal, administrative, financial, banking, capital, etc.

Clients

Society, community. Also other groups working in the same market, and other related groups. Formation of networks, associations, federations, movements, etc.

So, in the realm of working together, questions to consider are:

- How do we relate to our customers, suppliers, connected initiatives, bank, government, etc.? What style and form do we want to develop?
- How will we relate to our supporters, volunteers, benefactors, trustees, members of the Board? What style and form do we want to develop? What is the best legal form for our initiative?
- How do we want to organise ourselves? Who is deciding about what, and how do we reach decisions? What will be our approach to salaries?
- How willing are we to work on ourselves?

6. *Managing Processes and Time*

Have you ever been involved in a whole foods restaurant, or an organisation of adult classes, a toy-making workshop, or a bakery? In these initiatives you will see many of the co-workers very actively involved during the day running the work processes. The guest in the restaurant wants a warm, well prepared, well served meal. What has to happen for that is tremendous. Imagine you are the guest and look at the plate. How many ingredients are used in the meal, where do they come from, how did they arrive in the kitchen, how many people have been involved to make it possible that you can have this meal? If you really try to imagine this you will discover that many, many activities are interconnected, that everything we buy in a shop, or eat in a restaurant is the end result of incredibly complicated work processes.

You could say that the work processes are the lifeblood of the initiative. A constant transformation, an alchemy takes place, in which raw materials, hands, machines, human creativity, communication and time work together in such a way that the miracle happens time and again. In the history of the industrial revolution you can notice that much research has gone into the simplifying of work processes, giving to the machine those work processes that could be repeated. The result of this, however, was that workers had to follow the machines in repetitive, routine work.

This is not usually the experience of people when they start their enterprise. What you mostly see is a great talent to improvise; a dependency on the experience of one or two people who seem to be in charge of everything; constant pressure to deliver in time; chronic overwork to make ends meet. As a result, you see a lot of life and activity, but no rhythm. Often it looks to me as if the initiative is running out of breath; showing signs of hyperventilation. Many people in initiatives suffer from the lack of rhythm, the feeling that nothing can be finished, the constant pressure.

So there seems to be a great need to pay some attention to the running of the work processes so they can provide a rhythm to the activity, and be run most efficiently. For example, a farmer once told me that he was always having difficulties with the yogurt-making on the farm. So I asked him to write down what activities had to be done, in which order, to make the yogurt. I asked him: 'Try to think through the process from the moment the milk leaves the cow to the moment the yogurt carton is sold'. A week later he told me that by writing all these activities down he had already noticed that two or three things could be done better and faster. He gave this list to an artist who was interested in these processes with the question: 'Can you make these processes visible so that the yogurt maker, the apprentices and other helpers can look at it and know what has to be done next?' (See picture on the next page.)

Work processes need to be thought through with great care but also observed and regularly reviewed after the initiative has started. During the preparation one will realise that everything cannot be done at once and that it is necessary to set priorities. It is fantastic *to do* many things together and the better prepared people are, the more they are able to

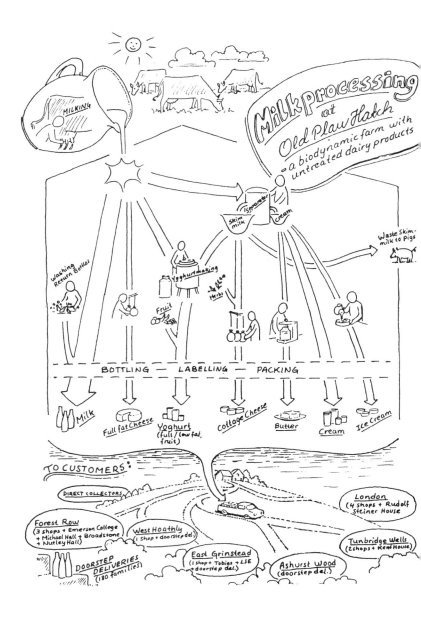

understand each other with half a word. But time *to review,* to take stock, to breathe, to keep people and ship on course has to be set aside and planned.

Questions to nurture this aspect are:

- Which work processes are needed to do the work and how can they be organised in the most effective way?
- What are our priorities?
- How do we organise our work life? When do we meet? Who prepares what? Who co-ordinates all activities? Who is responsible for the planning board?

Exercise: Observing Work Processes

When a group of people working together in an initiative want to look at the way they organise their work processes, with the aim of making these more effective, it can be helpful for each person to answer the following questions:

1a) Whose needs does your work *directly* serve? (This may be an external client, or someone in the same organisation whose work is dependent on yours).

 b) How direct is your relation to this person/ people? How accurately and frequently are you able to check what they require of you?

2a) Who allocates tasks to you? To whom do you allocate tasks?

Continued

b) How directly orientated are these tasks to the needs of your actual 'clients'?

c) Does the way you spend your time reflect the priorities of your 'clients'?

3a) What patterns of communication, accountability and control are you involved in?

b) Where are these helpful in supporting and guiding your work, and where do you find them inadequate, obtrusive or irrelevant?

4a) What resources (physical, financial, personal) are available for your use?

b) Where are these adequate, inadequate or superfluous?

5a) How would you characterise the leadership style in your organisation? e.g. autocratic/democratic/bureaucratic/functional/individualistic etc.

b) Do you feel this style maximises the effectiveness of your work? If not, in which direction would it need to change?

c) Do you experience enough scope for your own initiative and innovation?

6) (To be discussed with colleagues): What concrete steps could we take in any of these areas to enhance our effectiveness?

7. *Finding Facilities and Resources*

No initiative can start without a space (a room, a house, a building, a workshop), furniture, tools, materials and machines. Space can be bought or rented, furniture, tools and machines bought new or second hand. All can be renovated, decorated, or cleaned with the help of voluntary work, but in the end one needs to find a sum of money to finance the beginning of the initiative.

It is often a long search to find the right space and every initiative goes through endless deliberations to decide if they can afford the space or not. If you decide that this is the place, you have to go out and find the money. Many things need to be prepared for the bank, foundations, or close relatives of the initiative takers in order to come up with the necessary capital.

You have to describe the history, aims and proposed activities of the initiative (as described above under Formulating Direction) as well as describing in detail the possibilities of the space, the costs of renovation, and the value of the building if you want to buy it. The same applies to furniture, materials, tools, machinery. You often need to add to this personnel costs to make it possible for some of the future co-workers to have a salary at the beginning.

This is called the *investment budget,* in which you can even indicate the priorities and the times when these items must be financed.

In addition to the investment budget, every initiative must calculate the income and expenditure of the initiative in the first year and the expected growth over the next years, including the interest and repayment of capital. If you do this with great care and realism, with the help of an accountant or someone who is running a similar enterprise, it will become visible how much loan capital the initiative can carry and how much must be raised in gifts or venture capital. With these figures you can go to an established bank. If already available in your country, you could go to a bank institution like

Mercury Provident Society Plc, which specialises in helping new initiatives to raise the proper finances (see Chapter Five).[3] Together with such a bank you can create a fund-raising plan, making use of the bank's experience with different forms of raising gifts, establishing a borrowing community and finding personal guarantors.

If the initiative group has paid enough attention to the aspects described in this chapter it will be well received by the bank and can expect to work creatively with it.

Another aspect of the material foundation of the initiative is the care and artistic quality of the environment you are creating for the work. It does not have to be brand new or very modern, but you can do a lot with the choice of colour of the walls, flowers, cleaned and painted furniture. The space is the place where the co-workers will be every day for many hours; the place where you meet your customers, the school children, the guests, the students. It is the space where people breathe an atmosphere prepared with care and the touch of artistic quality can be experienced as a breath of fresh air in an overly functional world.

When preparing the facilities and looking for (or finding) the finances, ask yourself the following questions:

- What kind of space, environment and machinery do we need?
- What is our investment budget?
- What is our expected income and expenditure for the next two years?
- How much can we afford to borrow and how much must we raise in gifts?
- Who are the people, the institutions that could help us?
- What material do we have to prepare for the fund raising?
- What quality of environment do we want to offer to our customers and co-workers?

All of the above-mentioned seven basic aspects play a part in every initiative, and in already existing organisations or enterprises. Some of the aspects will be taken up more consciously than others; some are the focus of attention at a particular time. All have their place and together they form a totality. The first three aspects belong together and can penetrate with their light and quality in the more concrete and material aspects described in the last three aspects. In the middle stands the group of committed people, who are willing to take up the challenge, be creative, and use the initiative as a free space in which they can make a positive contribution to society.

*Starting and Nurturing Social
Initiatives: Checklist of Questions*

1   Recognising the Vision

Aim: To develop a sense of the motives which live
in the different initiative-takers.

- What do we want to realise in this
  initiative?
- Why is this also important to the other
  initiative-takers?
- What hopes, ideals, expectations could be
  realised?
- What changes would this bring to your
  life?
- How does this step relate to the rest of
  your biography?

When listening to the contributions of other
initiative-takers one can ask:

- What do we have in common and what
  differences do we have to accommodate?
- What is it that wants to live between us?
- What can we as an initiative-group make
  possible together? What can we not real-
  ise on our own?
- What is the identity of our work?
- What can we make possible together?

Continued

2 Answering a Need

Aim: Trying to creep in the skin of the customer

- Have we been and are we listening, observing and asking our customers what they expect? How are we going about that?
- What do people really express as their needs? How do we know that the initiative is needed?
- What needs, expectations do people express that could be incorporated in the initiative or even give it a change of emphasis?
- What opportunities and what restrictions lie in the situation one meets?
- Are people willing and able to pay a price for our services?

And more general:

- What are trends, signals of the time and is the initiative a response to them?

3 Formulating direction

Aim: To develop a living picture of how the initiative will function in 2 or 3 years
Make a brochure to express:

- The name of the initiative.

Continued

       — Artistic representations of a central aspect of the name or the activities of the initiative.

       — A short description of the history, the motive, the general aims, and main activities.

Try further to describe:

       — What co-workers want to have achieved within the next 2 or 3 years, what activities will be developed.

       — The basic style, the basic attitude of working within the initiative. The house style in relation to customers, co-workers, community, suppliers, financiers, etc.

4   Commitment of people

Aim: To find the network of people that will nurture and support the initiative

       — What criteria do you want to use when to find your potential colleagues, supporters, or volunteers?

       — What risks are people willing and able to take?

       — Is there enough patience, endurance, courage, ambition in the group to succeed?

       — Who will be the carriers, who are the supporters?

Continued

– What personal investments of others (dependents) or resources of others are we risking with this step?

5 *Working together*

Aim: To describe the way you are to organise the initiative

– How do we want to organise ourselves? How will we communicate, when will we meet, who is deciding about what?
– How will we relate to our supporters, volunteers, benefactors, trustees, members of the Board?
– What is the best legal form for our initiative?
– How will we approach the question of salaries?
– How willing are we to work on ourselves?

6 *Managing processes and time*

Aim: To observe and describe the work processes that make the initiative fulfil its task.

– Which work processes are needed to do the work and how can they be organised in the most effective way?
– What are our priorities?
– How will we organise the work life? What different functions have to be taken care of? Who will co-ordinate the activities?

Continued

Who is responsible for the planning board?

7   *Finding facilities and resources*

Aim: To build a realistic picture of the facilities and financial needs of the initiative.

- What kind of space, environment, machinery, etc., do we need?
- What quality of environment do we want to offer to our customers and co-workers?
- What is our investment budget?
- What is our expected income and expenditure for the next two years?
- How much can we afford to borrow and how much can we raise in gifts?
- Who are the people, the institutions that could help us?
- What material do we have to prepare for the fund raising?

Why do Initiatives Fail?

Problem Diagnosis Using The 'Seven Steps'

1. Recognising the Motive

- loss of enthusiasm after 'honeymoon' period.
  - loss of energy when routine sets in or obstacles encountered.
  - loss of direction of long-term aims, constantly compromised to adapt to circumstances.
  - unrealistic, overambitious schemes.

2. Answering a Need

- losing touch with changing requirements.
  - preoccupation with internal management reduces client/customer orientation.
  - failure to maintain effective promotion and research.

3. Formulating Direction

- falling quality.
  - obsolescence.

Continued

– overtaken by competitors.
– price no longer attractive.

4. *Commitment of People*

– skills not adequate.
– effort too low or misdirected.
– avoidance of risk – missed opportunities.

5. *Organisation of Relationships*
   – Working Together

– inappropriate legal structure.
– failure to make clear agreements re. ownership control, decision-making profit sharing, interpersonal conflicts, poor communication.
– inappropriate leadership style/lack of leadership.
– bureaucracy – reduced motivation of staff.

6. *Managing Processes and Time*

– lack of effective work – planning and supervision.
Inefficiencies due to:
– poor equipment/facilities,
– purchasing policy,
– production methods,
– distribution methods,
– admin. procedures.

Continued

- lack of feedback information re. costs/benefits.
- inflexibility of processes in response to changed needs.

7. Finding Resources and Facilities

- under-capitalisation, inadequate financial control,
- waste,
- shortages of key supplies.

34

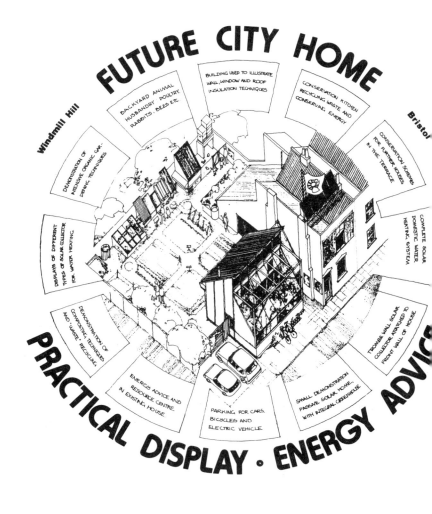

FUTURE CITY HOME

Windmill Hill

Bristol

BUILDING USED TO ILLUSTRATE WALL, WINDOW AND ROOF INSULATION TECHNIQUES

BACKYARD ANIMAL HUSBANDRY. POULTRY, RABBITS, BEES ETC.

CONSERVATION KITCHEN RECYCLING WASTE AND CONSERVING ENERGY

DEMONSTRATION OF INTENSIVE ORGANIC GAR-DENING TECHNIQUES

CONSERVATION SCHEMES FOR FURTHER HOUSES IN THE TERRACE

DISPLAYS OF DIFFERENT TYPES OF SOLAR COLLECTOR FOR WATER HEATING.

COMPLETE SOLAR DOMESTIC WATER HEATING SYSTEM

DEMONSTRATION OF COMPOSTING TECHNIQUES AND "WASTE" RECYCLING.

TROMBE WALL SOLAR COLLECTOR ATTACHED TO FRONT WALL OF HOUSE

ENERGY ADVICE AND RESOURCE CENTRE IN EXISTING HOUSE

SMALL DEMONSTRATION PASSIVE SOLAR HOME WITH INTEGRAL GREENHOUSE

PARKING FOR CARS, BICYCLES AND ELECTRIC VEHICLE.

PRACTICAL DISPLAY · ENERGY ADVICE

UCAT: Formulating Direction

Chapter Two

Getting Going: The Growing Pains and Childhood Diseases of Initiatives

Tijno Voors

Many legends describe the story of a young person going out into the world. There are many trials and temptations. There are obstacles to overcome, tasks to carry out in order to successfully complete the journey.

This also happens with new initiatives. Initiatives often go through a long period of trial and error before they establish themselves in the world. Starting an initiative is meeting a challenge, is taking a step into the unknown. In changing something in an existing organisation, or in starting something new, you meet resistances. No initiative can come to full maturity without going through a process of learning and development. Trials and temptations are outwardly experienced as forces that want to destroy the initiative, as forms of illness. Inwardly they can be seen as forces of resistance which, if met and learned from, can create a stronger group of people, more able to meet the tasks at hand.

This chapter describes some of the trials and temptations which new initiatives face. They are drawn from the experience of the Triodos Bank in Holland. Alexander Bos, one of the members of the Triodos group, was able to recognise and describe a number of these.[1]

One useful perspective from which to view the challenges that face new initiatives is that of childhood illnesses. These are to some degree inevitable and seem to strengthen the child, allowing its individuality to emerge more clearly. Yet it is important to know something of these illnesses in order to be able to treat them. The same can be said of the challenges or illnesses of new initiatives. They cannot be altogether avoided; they serve to strengthen the initiative if overcome, but it is important to know something about them before starting off on the journey.

'A Silver Spoon'

Everyone who has seen an initiative almost die for lack of funds knows the seductive thought, 'If only we could get a legacy of twenty-thousand from somewhere, our problems would be solved'. One starts to think about Uncle George or Aunt Nellie – they have given so generously to that other initiative. Isn't it our turn now? Another wished for 'uncle' can be the Government, the Manpower Services, or a large foundation.

In fact, one large donation or the total subsidising of an initiative can be one of the worst things that can happen. It looks as if the time is now, the ideals can become reality, talking is over, we can start. I can still remember how impressed I was when I first entered a new shop, a nicely decorated large former theatre. You could walk from one section to another, and buy your vegetables, groceries, books, toys, pure wool and clothes, etc. You could wander from one place to another and marvel at the quality and the taste. Prices were stiff, but things were very well presented. On the 'stage' was a coffee corner and an exhibition. Marvellous. Within a year there were serious financial problems; supply and stock had to be drastically limited. The space looked empty, too big. The 'spoon', the beautiful theatre-space, had proved to be too good and too expensive.

Similar things happen when someone offers an initiative a beautiful building for a school, or a medical centre, when it is just starting. The same can happen when one receives a substantial sum of money to start a series of publications on a very important subject. However, after two issues the money is gone. Where are the buyers to finance the next?

What is happening, or not happening, in this situation? One has seemingly received an answer to the question whether the initiative is really needed. An initial donation, gift, subsidy, or legacy has made a big step possible. But clients, patients, students, need to guarantee an initiative's continued existence. This is tested only over time. If they are not coming to buy after an initial show of interest; if they do not become regular readers; if only a few children come to the school; then one has to ask oneself: 'Was the initiative really needed?'

We have seen in Chapter One how important it is to answer a need, to find recognition and support for the initiative in its immediate environment. When there is no large gift, no fine building, no good spoon, then the initiative-takers have to engage themselves in the long and often tiresome tasks of finding many gifts, and a variety of supporters. That means meeting people, talking about the initiative, in order to make people enthusiastic about its aims and hopes.

Such effort creates new realities. The initiative group is forced to go beyond the small and immediate circle of friends. This strengthens their sense of purpose, their clarity of aim, and helps them to develop a real dialogue with the environment. To be forced to articulate the essential aspects of the initiative can also help to make visible the fact that different members of the group have quite different pictures of the initiative. You can discover this when you meet with people and listen how the other is speaking about plans for the future. Sometimes you can have the feeling: 'Is he really talking about the same thing?'. To experience this can often help to face differences at an early stage, thereby avoiding a difficult conflict later on.

To interest many into giving small amounts creates much more than the sum total of these small gifts. Small gifts often come from a warm heart. Large subsidies, legacies, or grants are often quite cold. One does not have to refuse them, but they do not create the mantle of warmth, so important for a small infant.

Fund-raising activities are good feelers for finding out if the initiative is wanted. The initiative-takers need to speak to people who will benefit from the idea. The results of such activities may be so minimal that it works like a cold shower. Not very nice, but reality needs to be looked at, if there is not much support.

Grand Propaganda

Over many years an idea had been living in his mind. The idea had grown and grown, almost to the exclusion of everything else. This idea simply had to become reality. Many people were waiting for this initiative to be realised. The ideal building and grounds were found and brochures were sent all over Europe. Many people were talking about this grand idea and were inspired. It touched something they had been waiting for. Some came, selling their property to help to finance this new venture. Others came because they had heard about it and expected that they could start a new life. There were large meetings to discuss the future and all the work that had to be done. People worked on the buildings, and moved in. But people need to be fed, to be paid, and to live. Gradually questions appeared:

- Were all these people really needed to prepare for the task?
- Who was responsible for feeding everyone?

- Who should handle the money?
- Where were the resources to be found to help the initiative through the preparation period?
- Was everyone deciding everything together? Or did all depend on the initiator, the pioneer, the owner, and the financier?

Nothing dramatic happened, but gradually people left. Money that was promised did not materialise. Money borrowed for a short period was asked back. Feelings of deception, defeat, disappointment, and anger arose. Mutual accusations abounded. The window that people had been looking through into a potentially beautiful garden had shattered.

In this example a number of difficulties can be recognised. One of them is that a person or a group of people fall in love with their own idea. They cannot think of anything else, and the feeling grows stronger every day that they are chosen to bring this idea into reality. The group says: 'It is very clear that the world is waiting for us, waiting for this idea. We want to bring good to the world with our idea'. Ideas often have a strong influence on people, even to the degree that they can possess individuals. It is possible to live so strongly with an idea that one loses the ability to observe what reality needs to be created, and what is actually called for. Perception is distorted and a dialogue with the environment is missing.

It is like Narcissus, a figure from mythology. He discovers his image in a lake and falls in love with it. This also happens with ideas and ideals. Self-love creeps into them and observation gets obscured. Difficulties are multiplied. When other people draw attention to some of the consequences, they are ignored, or told that they do not understand the true nature of the initiative. Questions are regarded as hostile and supporters who wish to help realistically are labelled 'Adversaries'. Symptoms of fanaticism, paranoia and martyrdom begin to appear.

The above example also shows us another childhood disease. We spoke about the need for every initiative to find recognition and support in its environment. Some people, however, have the gift to speak and communicate in such a way that potential co-workers, supporters, givers are immediately taken in by the beauty of the possibilities. Such individuals can awaken support in people, and affect their independent judgement. However, the gold tongue – good propaganda – often leaves a bad taste, a sense of being cheated if the initiative was not grounded and the information given not true.

The beautiful idea, and the gift of persuasion can both serve to hinder a genuine dialogue with people about what is really needed and what they want to do and to support; while both of these qualities are needed, in excess they work as a drug which blocks hard work and the necessary realism.

Do It All Yourself

An initiative can experience a quite different illness when people think they have to do it all by themselves, with no external help. Being independent, running one's own show, being self-supporting and autonomous becomes the motto. You hear the sentiment expressed: 'An initiative that has some self-respect should be able to carry itself from the start'.

This means in practice that an initiative group goes to a bank to borrow the necessary amount for capital and start-up cost. At best they try to get a lower interest rate. As a consequence they often have to start paying interest before the initiative has properly been launched, and a proportion of the loan will have to be repaid after half a year or a year. The question arises whether financing of this kind is appropriate in the early stages. It may be that a combination of gifts and loans is better, depending on what kind of initiative it is.

Through excessive self-reliance and early over-borrowing a number of initiatives that Triodos worked with ran into difficulties. One example was a group of people who wanted to start a whole-food restaurant. They had imagined that the restaurant would pay for itself within the first year. The calculation worked out on paper: 'So many meals and so many drinks for such a price makes such and such an income.'

Reality, of course, was different. It takes at least a year before a restaurant has found its place in the neighbourhood. It takes a while before customers have found their way to the restaurant; the quality of food, meetings, types of people, and atmosphere all need to be experienced. Actual costs are normally higher than expected, and income less than hoped for.

Another example known to the author was a bookstore in the United States which started with a large bank loan at high interest. While it was reasonably successful it struggled with this loan for its entire existence – thereby not having the possibility of expanding into the cultural activities which the initiators wanted.

It lies in the nature of things that new initiatives need the help of free gifts to make a good start. Gifts also make visible if the initiative is really wanted. Because they are free, one does not begin with a heavy obligation to be financially successful from the start. New developments need to spread their wings. Gifts make this possible. Later on, loans for a new building or for expansion are right because the initiative is established and known.

The Ideal Model

Some initiatives are hindered in their development because they start with a fully worked out structure and form. A foundation is created to own future buildings and to deal with future surpluses. A Limited Liability Company, complete with directors and an advisory Board, a totally worked out organisation chart with functional descriptions, scheduled meetings, and procedures. Even income and expenditure accounts are projected for the next three years, but all before any actual activity has started.

What is really happening here? People are creating legal, organisational, and social forms, without content. Much thought and deliberation have gone into this organisation structure. Co-workers, board members, even customers are somehow expected to feel at ease in these neatly designed forms. The reality is often the reverse. Co-workers experience a dogmatism which hinders free initiative and organic development. It is as if these structure-creators have given up on life. True observation of life shows us that life creates its own forms. The stream will create its own bed. Living activity and development shows what form it needs. Form and movement must enter into a conversation. Some form, of course, is needed in the early stages of an initiative, but the right form for a particular initiative has to evolve gradually out of the work – out of the flow of activities.

Over-organisation can appear because of the desire for security or from ideological models. The Co-operative model, The Participative Community model, The Egalitarian model, and The Waldorf School model are only a few examples. Ideals and values are of course important and should be reflected in structures, but an early over-emphasis runs the risk that dogma becomes both authority and reality, and people and the initiative the means to realise it.

The Absent Initiative Taker

A similar difficulty can be experienced when someone has a brilliant idea, but others have to execute it. Here one can see the temptation of expecting others to realise your dream, to nurture your infant initiative.

This happened in the following situation. Someone had observed the need to create a Centre for drug addicts, which would use a therapeutic approach involving, medical, artistic, and biographical help. Only the co-workers were absent. A group was found after some initial struggle. This group realised the idea, but the person whose idea it was could not just follow it from a distance and help with counsel when asked. Instead, he interfered every time the initiative went in a direction that did not coincide with his ideas or expectations. Inevitably this led to great tension and ultimately to a break in the relationship, leaving bad feelings all round.

The Negative Umbrella

Over the last ten to fifteen years, more and more parents have questioned the quality of comprehensive State education. They were not happy with the education but did not want to, or could not afford to, send their children to private boarding schools. However, they wanted an 'alternative' school. Often they had heard that elsewhere groups of parents were founding Steiner Schools, and they decided to do something similar.

They would often start by finding a house or empty school, cleaning it, and decorating it. Small chairs and desks were acquired from a school that had just closed. A Foundation was formed with a Board of strong enthusiastic parents, and with lots of effort a teacher was found to take the first class. Quite a number of parents had been waiting for this and decided to send their children. The school started, invited friends and the community for an Open Day, and everyone was excited and happy.

However, even during the start-up period in such a school, certain misunderstandings and tensions can become evident, but the enthusiasm to create an alternative form of education prevails. Gradually it dawns on the initiative-takers that they have found each other *through the rejection of the old*, but their views of the alternative, of the positive and new, are very different. Everyone has their own concept of the alternative, often related to their own values of education and child-rearing. Under the Negative Umbrella of the Alternative

School people have found each other, but signs of disintegration rapidly appear.

This phenomenon was, for example, very apparent in the United States in the late Sixties and early Seventies, when alternative 'free' schools sprang up overnight, but few of them survived for more than a year or two. The causes of conflict are varied. Some parents expect the school to be democratic; parents and children must be able to participate and decide on all aspects of the school's life. Others have come because they expect an anti-authoritarian approach. 'When I was in school I felt like a branch of a tree that was constantly pruned. Every time a new branch started to grow it was clipped by the teacher. I want my daughter to be in a school where she can unfold herself freely. She knows best what is good for her own development'.

Again, others have participated in the founding of the school because they want their child to have a proper Steiner education. It is a painful process when these inevitable discussions about principles, background, world view, and views on child development take place after the school has already started. The central question then becomes: 'Can these different elements tolerate each other, and can the teachers find a firm foundation to work on.'

There are, of course, people in such a group who say: 'Let's be tolerant – all the different ways of looking at education have their validity. Indeed, they complement each other.' However, this is not practical, as the inevitable compromises lead either to a colourless educational experiment or to the withdrawal of everyone's support. It is a misplaced form of tolerance which says: 'We all want to work for a better education. So let's throw all the different approaches together and choose the best part of each.'

In cultural life different approaches, different points of view, different spiritual orientations need to have the possibility of expressing their own colour, their own identity; otherwise their unique contributions cannot become visible.

This does not happen only with new approaches to

education, but in colleges, training centres, alternative workshops for young unemployed, and consultancy groups, to name just a few examples. The same can be said for therapeutic and medical centres, where a number of alternative therapeutic and medical approaches try to work together. The attempted fusion of differences based on a negative motivation seldom works. It is therefore best to be clear about what you stand for, as well as what you do not like, before the initiative begins.

The Power of Routine

Real initiatives are always in conflict with daily reality. As long as an initiative is on its way to being born, the initial spirit, the enthusiasm, and determination to battle on, keep the group on its toes.

But the moment the shop, the school, the workshop or the restaurant, is in business, the reality of daily life demands attention. Daily, repetitive routine work has to be done. There is no time for meetings with the co-workers because the customers, clients, parents, patients and the bank manager must be kept happy. There seems to be time only for work and responsibility.

With this, one gradually loses touch with the source, and the power of the initiative decreases. The spirit out of which the initiative was born is no longer being renewed. Instead, daily routine work takes over. An initiative that does not find time to review its work, to reconnect with the inspiration, to create a space where co-workers can share their questions and experiences, will gradually lose all sense of renewal.

So, as the initiative grows and becomes well established, the need for reflection, for renewal, for stepping out of the everyday, becomes a vital necessity. One could say that a time for reconnecting with the initial vision is needed so that a dialogue with the original motivating spirit can occur.

Too Rapid Growth

There is also a danger in too much success. A new store starts, and all of a sudden the orders come in so quickly that a more orderly growth process becomes impossible. A store in Montreal selling cotton mattresses started selling direct to customers in street markets and through direct orders. It soon began to grow so that a manufacturing and retail operation was required. The initiators felt as if they were chasing cotton down a hillside but hardly gaining on it. Such experiences are quite common and can lead to stress, confusion, and a feeling of being overwhelmed. Like the demands of routine, the demands of excessive growth can obscure original intentions and lead the initiative in unwanted directions. The pressures of hiring, training, book-keeping, supervising, ordering, and selling can become too much. Here too a pause, a period of reflection, is required and a setting of priorities so that the relative chaos can still reflect something of the earlier intentions.

We have discussed some of the typical trials that new initiatives face in the early phases of their development. The list of trials, of childhood diseases, is of course not complete. You may, out of your experience, describe others such as the Know it all Pioneer, the Perfect but Unwanted Product, or the Overstaffed and Overoptimistic school. What is important is to recognise that these trials or illnesses are to a greater or lesser extent inevitable and that if they are met and worked on they lead to greater health for the initiative, and more understanding and self-knowledge for the initiative takers. If the attitude of learning from successes and failures, if gaining new insights from experience prevails then the initiative will live, and the infant has a good chance of growing to maturity.

The Dragons

Another way of describing the struggles of initiatives is to see an army of dragons trying to devour the new born initiative. Where these dragons fail, the initiative becomes purified, reinforced and socially fruitful.

1. *The Disintegration Dragon*
   Many initiative-takers have found each other through rejection of the old, but their views of the alternative, of the positive, are often different. Differences in motives, basic orientations, expectations of the members of the initiative can very soon lead to disintegration.

2. *The Sect Dragon*
   An initiative must always guard itself against the temptation of blindly believing in having found the pure motive. If this happens it withdraws in sect-like self-sufficiency.

3. *The Silver Spoon or Subsidy Dragon*
   The large gift at the start can prevent the initiative from working for its recognition in the environment. Lack of money might mean that the initiative is not ready to be born yet, or has no reason to exist at all.

4. *The Autonomy or 'Go it Alone' Dragon*
   Some people think they can do it all by themselves, with no external help. Being independent, being self-supporting and auton-

Continued

omous, becomes the motto. 'An initiative that has some self-respect should be able to carry itself from the start'. But actual costs are normally higher than expected, and income less than hoped for.

5. *Adapting Dragon*
   'Let's be tolerant — all the different ways of looking at education / therapy etc. have their validity!' This is however not always practical, because the inevitable compromise leads either to a colourless experiment or to the withdrawal of everyone's support.

6. *Ideal Model Dragon*
   Starting with a fully worked out structure of 'The Co-operative Model', 'The Egalitarian Model', 'The Free School Model', etc. can work extremely dogmatically and will hinder free initiative and organic development.

7. *The Absent Initiative-Taker Dragon or Delegation Dragon*
   Someone has a brilliant idea, but others have to execute it. It is the temptation to expect others to realise one's dream, especially when a group takes the initiative, but the initiator continues giving instructions to the executors.

8. *The Solo Dragon*
   The pioneer can be so strong that others are prevented from feeling co-responsibility. The danger is that the initiative becomes one-sided

Continued

and dependent on the pioneer alone, with a nice bunch of followers. The initiative can very rapidly disappear with the father figure.

9. *The Hurry Dragon*
Just like babies, initiatives need time for maturing, for incubation. The hurry dragon whispers to us that this is the hour to act, to start, and not sit back and contemplate. In this way premature births come about which will suffer an early death.

10. *The Expansion Dragon or Too Rapid Growth Dragon*
Some initiatives seem so relevant that they are threatened by expansive growth. But growth asks for new co-workers with adequate capabilities and for rapid organisational changes, otherwise the initiative grows itself to pieces.

11. *The Dilettante Dragon*
Every initiative needs capable people, willing to learn and to develop themselves. The dilettante dragon whispers to us continuously in the ear that we can stay as the one we are already. The result is a 'nice' initiative with a bunch of well-meaning amateurs.

12. *The Routine Dragon*
Every initiative is in conflict with daily reality. Repetitive routine work has to be done. The danger is that one gradually loses touch with the source. The daily routine takes over.

Continued

13. *False Economy Dragon*
'When the motive is right, the need is expressed, the money will come – so let's start'. John
knows someone who can install the central
heating and Peter has some furniture and we
can live with the draft etc. One hears the 'false
economy dragon' laughing. When mid-winter
comes, the pipes burst, the furniture falls to
pieces and the school has to close for a few
weeks.

14. *The Bursar Dragon*
'We can only spend when the money is
received'. 'We haven't budgetted for this, so
we cannot do it'. The danger of this dragon is
that every initiative is killed before it is born
because there is no money.

These dragons can be placed in pairs and related to
the seven aspects described in Chapter One.

1. Recognising the Motive
The Disintegration Dragon   The Sect Dragon

2. Answering a Need
The Subsidy Dragon   The Autonomy Dragon

3. Formulating Direction
The Adapting Dragon   The Model Dragon

4. Commitment of People
The Delegation Dragon   The Solo Dragon

Continued

5. Working Together
The Hurry Dragon   The Expansion Dragon

6. Managing Processes and Time
The Dilettante Dragon   The Routine Dragon

7. Finding Resources and Facilities
The False Economy Dragon   The Bursar Dragon

Many of these dragons surround an initiative and they will make use of any weakness. At the same time they are the development helpers – just as childhood illnesses – of the initiative.

This picture of the dragons can be used as a diagnostic tool by the co-workers to enable them to become clear about the challenges that face them. It might be helpful to spend an evening together looking at the one-sidedness of one's initiative and discussing how consciousness and balance can be brought into the situation.

Case Study: Hearthstone Community Association
Ross Jennings

Hearthstone, located in Wilton, New Hampshire (USA), is a group of eleven families who lease a 92 acre tract of land from the Monadnock Community Land Trust. The 99 year lease pledges the membership of Hearthstone to using and developing the land in an ecologically responsible manner. Hearthstone's relationship to the land trust bears witness to its intention of being a steward to the land and to break the chain of treatment of land as a commodity by removing it from the speculative market.

About seven years ago, the group that evolved into Hearthstone came together to consider the dilemma posed to the Wilton area by the proposed sale of a farm where Bio-dynamic agriculture was becoming established. While the owner did not wish to see this beginning go to naught, circumstances were forcing him to put the farm on the open market by September 1978, unless some alternative could be found.

That was the question which faced the group that gathered on August 17, 1978. As one member of that original group, my expectations were not very high – perhaps an 'angel' could be found – but at the very least we would have the satisfaction of having tried to save the farm. As we introduced ourselves, it suddenly became apparent that alongside our concern for the land we had common interests in 'community' and individually affordable housing.

Then it was clear that the synthesis of these concerns and interests was leading us to the conclusion that *we* should buy the farm! In the enthusiasm engendered by this discovery each individual openly shared his or her financial capabilities – (i.e., what could be applied to a down payment, what could be contributed to servicing a mortgage). This was a very amazing experience as several of the people gathered didn't know one another previously.

Thus began a process that was to come to mean meeting every week for the first three and a half years. Our individual 'obsessions' ranged from homesteading, to windmills, to methane digesters. What became increasingly clear from the outset was the necessity of finding a process that insured that each person's interest could be shared, valued and respected and that together we had to find the next practical and achievable step. Frequently what appeared to be outer obstacles, such as the complex process for the approval of the project by the town of Wilton, turned out to be a blessing as we were given deadlines to meet, questions to answer, and the responsibility of making our lofty collective vision comprehensible to the 'powers that be'! Our work with the town of Wilton is a testament to the value of openness, trust and clarity. A mutual respect was formed during this process as we sometimes had to compromise.

With the farm saved, the door was open to start a community building project. The process of building up a shared vision of our 'intentionally created neighbourhood' was both challenging and fascinating. Our age range (8 – 80), varied backgrounds (New Hampshire native, Georgists, Parisian Cosmopolite) and work experiences (teachers, builders, artists, publisher, retired cop) always made for a lively exchange. After a while, we realised that our real strength lay in our diversity and that as our individual capacities grew to accept and be tolerant of perspectives different from our own the 'efficiency' of our work was enhanced. This learning process – stretched over three and a half years of meeting every week – was punctuated by crises that could not be met unless the group was continuously willing to raise its 'trust threshold.' An important turning point in our work together came in a meeting where we acknowledged that a cornerstone of our work together was to 'take on the development of the other.' We agreed to be open to one another, and to have the courage to share our feelings and perceptions freely.

One element that has helped us greatly was the inclusion of a short evaluation period as part of each meeting. We began this in the early days of clearing the land as we found it important to set aside time to reflect on the day's work – not only to become more skilful at the tasks but to mend any tears in our social fabric. The opportunity of working together over a prolonged period gave us a refined sense of the nuances of the consensus decision-making process – it's always too slow for one or too fast for the other.

We have found it essential to respect the laws that govern the functioning of our three-fold nature as human beings. We come together once or twice a year to look at the question: 'Who are we and where are we going?' These 'non-business' meetings are important for clearing the air and redefining our work in light of what's possible at any given moment. With a sizable group, over a long period of time conditions arise which create the challenge of living with a panorama of personal crises. Learning how to objectify and to transform personal upset into opportunity for development for the individual and the group is a goal we have acknowledged as central to our work together.

As the project grows over time, change comes in its wake. New members join, new life responsibilities emerge and as one phase of the work together is completed new levels of function must come forth to meet the new challenges. Initially the tasks were fairly straightforward: clearing and stacking wood, building roads, creating a site plan, and working with the town and state authorities. We were very fortunate in these early stages in finding people with necessary professional skills who could provide their services without denying our members the opportunity to contribute. In the end new skills were tapped within the group: a former stage designer produced beautiful site plan drawings, a former teacher dowsed for water, and the responsibility for managing the project became widely shared.

After this beginning phase, individual leaseholders gradually shifted to the awesome task of designing and building their own homes. At present eleven families are living on the land with homes in varying stages of completion. Building a house for most people is a microcosm of the manic-depressive syndrome – wild swings between elation and depression and the discovery that your world horizon has shrunk to a few millimeters' span. Sharing this 'rite of passage' with other fellow travelers was sometimes a return ticket to sanity.

For the first couple of years our meetings were the only time we saw one another. Now other forms of social contact are gradually evolving. We share festival times together (where individually possible) and include in our meetings time for personal sharing. Purely social occasions – pot-luck desserts, pancake breakfasts, singing, games, etc. – are a way of meeting prospective new members and to reach out into the larger community.

We have felt from the outset that Hearthstone has a larger purpose than providing low cost housing opportunities for its members. Much favorable publicity about the project has brought a stream of visitors who are interested in a working example of land trust principles. For the future we envision additional land being cleared for fields and other community buildings. One idea that we are working with would be to create a multi-functional facility: a gathering place for Hearthstone (we no longer easily fit in a single house), a setting for therapeutic work, and a place for workshops and lectures for the public. An indoor swimming pool that would also serve as a passive solar thermal mass is one of our favorite fantasies.

The development costs to date and the purchase monies are repaid through our lease fee which is also a proportionate share of the taxes, maintenance, insurance, and other running costs. We have so far been able to keep the lease fee affordable and as we add new members our capacity to afford additional development increases. An exciting dimension to the project has been the need to look beyond our membership for development monies. We have sponsored talks on the theme of socially beneficial investment and have worked with organisations such as the Revolving Loan Fund of the Institute for Community Economics.

In summary, I would describe Hearthstone as a living experiment in the relationship of inner and outer development. We have frequently found ourselves faced with decisions whose only reference point was our previous experience. This reminds me of the 'oral tradition' and folk wisdom of a tribal society. Our bond, however, is not of blood, but is based on conscious choice. The process together is a continual challenge to exercise our capacities as free individuals who associate to carry out our work for the common good. Our ideal as a working group is embodied in Rudolf Steiner's verse, 'The Social Ethic,' which we close our meetings with:

'The healthy social life is found when
in the mirror of the human soul the
whole community finds its reflection
and when in the community the virtue
of each one is living.'

Chapter Three

The Human Being and Organisational Forms

Christopher Schaefer

The Historical Context: Consciousness and Form

The art of working together needs to be consciously developed in our time if new initiatives are to grow in a healthy manner. Meeting this challenge, however, requires some understanding and appreciation of the human being and, in particular, insights into the kind of consciousness we have acquired in Western societies during the last centuries.

A hundred years ago there were few books on leadership, relationships, group facilitation, decision-making or communication. Most people lived in fairly closed communities in villages, extended families and small work communities. For many the world was circumscribed by tradition, church and family patterns. People more or less knew how to work and live together, usually out of tradition and habit. We had not yet become such a riddle to ourselves that bookshelves could be lined with psychological best sellers.

What has changed? What happened to human beings and

to society? While the answer is complex and has historical roots going back into the Middle Ages and beyond, one could say that today we stand at a point of maximum individualization, with powers like God over man and nature.[1] Science and technology have given us the possibility of preserving or destroying the earth and ourselves. Religious codes, community mores and family patterns are less and less binding. We live in a culture in which what 'I think', 'I feel' and 'I want' is of paramount importance. This is particularly true of the 'me first' culture in North America, aided by marketing appeals, images of instant gratification, and an educational system which tends to foster the values of taking care of oneself.

The positive side of this development is that we have the possibility of increased self understanding and choice. What do I really think – what is right and not right? What values do I wish to pursue in life? What profession and lifestyle should I choose? Endless choices and possibilities! One could say the individual increasingly has the possibility of acting out of freedom and out of a new self-awareness.

The negative aspect of this picture, in addition to the continued exploitation of the earth and of people, is that we are cut off from each other and from the earth. We are like hermits walking through the world because an increased awareness of self, of my thoughts, feelings and intentions, means I am less aware of others. Self awareness is initially bought at the price of pronounced anti-social, self centered qualities as anyone dealing with teenagers has noticed. We live in an age where the anti-social forces of self consciousness are starkly evident in increased divorce rates, family conflicts and social misunderstandings in the home and in the workplace.

One of the essential antidotes to the anti-social nature of the times is the creation of new life and work communities in which people are encouraged to build bridges between each other based on a conscious recognition of interdependence. And in many places we do see individuals making such an effort to build bridges. Bridges between the world of matter and the world of spirit, bridges to narrow the gap between free individuals and bridges of new consciousness and respect for the earth. This implies turning our consciousness outward, using our thinking, feeling and willing to perceive others and the needs of the earth. It is a tremendous step in which new initiatives can play a vital role by challenging our self-consciousness to be other directed.[2] This stretching of consciousness, this necessary inter-relationship between the individual and the community is clearly described by Rudolf Steiner in his motto of the social ethic:

> The healthy social life is only found when in the mirror of the human soul the whole community finds its reflection and when in the community the virtue of each one is living.[3]

Realising something of these ideals requires a new understanding of ourselves, of initiatives and organisations as human creations and continuous practice in forms of working together.

The Human Being as an Image of Organisational Life

If we realise that organisations are created by people for people, then one of the questions which arises is out of what model or metaphor are these institutions created? Is it an input-output model, a closed mechanical system, a biological metaphor or a living image of the human being? We, like Berger and Luckman, think that all initiatives, all institutions consciously or unconsciously reflect the value preferences and ultimately the image of the human being of the initiative takers.[4] If this is the case then it matters what image is explicitly or implicitly chosen and what such an image tells us about organisational life and about forms of working together.

While there are many possible images of the human being, our starting point is to see man linked to both a physical world and a spiritual world, while experiencing life psychologically through the medium, or on the stage, of the soul. This picture of the human being has been thoroughly and sensitively described by Zeylmans van Emmichoven, the Dutch psychiatrist, and can be checked against one's own experience. In its most basic form this picture does not substantially differ from that of Jung, Assagioli or that of many humanistic psychologists.

Zeylmans describes the soul as a stage on which we both experience ourselves and the world (both physical and spiritual). Through our physical body we experience the world of matter and through our higher eternal being (ego) we are connected to the eternal world of the spirit. Our soul faculties of thought, feeling and will (doing) allow us to both digest experiences and to independently interact with the spiritual, social and natural environment. Seen diagrammatically, the following picture emerges:

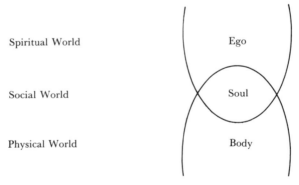

Spiritual World	Ego
Social World	Soul
Physical World	Body

This sketch of human nature is of course incomplete. It is a spatial representation ignoring the phases of human development from birth, through childhood, into adulthood and old age. It also does not do justice to the uniqueness of each individual, the richness of each personality in its life development. Yet it can serve as the basis for a better understanding of the ways of working together in initiatives and gives us clues about relevant questions and distinctions to pursue.

Three Realms of Organisational Life

The seven aspects that need to be nurtured in every initiative as described in Chapter One are pictured in the following diagram:

We can distinguish in this three distinct realms of organisational life. One realm is the 'body' – the building, the office furniture, the discreet work tasks and the money received and spent to keep the initiative alive. In a manufacturing organisation this level of activity is the most obvious and receives the bulk of attention; for example the making of engines, furniture or lamps and the maintenance of equipment and buildings. In a school or therapeutic centre it is less pronounced as the focus of activity is on the learning or healing process but the bodily level is still important as it provides the basis for existence.

A second realm of the initiative is that of 'soul', the quality and nature of relationships between people and the principles, policies and systems which guide those relationships. How are working conditions defined? What salary arrangements are there? What is the style of leadership and communication? On walking into a store, college or an office a mood can be sensed from the way in which people talk to each other, how they work and how they view each other.

A third realm is that of 'spirit', or identity. This level is difficult to describe as it is embodied in the initiative's culture, its vision, the needs it serves, the goals, history and name. What makes the Barnabas Project in Detroit different from Shire Training Workshops in Stroud, England? Both work with young unemployed. Why does one get a different feeling from one school than another even if they are based on the same educational philosophy? The vision, the context, the people – all of these certainly play a role, yet they only constitute the more visible expression of identity, of the spirit which lives in and through an initiative.

A Typology of Initiatives

It is not only important to ask questions about the basic realms of organisational life in order to develop appropriate forms of working together but also to reflect on the aims or goals different types of institutions pursue. A community college is clearly different from an automobile company or a hospital and must evolve forms in keeping with its aims of fostering the educational process.

If we look at cultural institutions such as schools, churches, colleges, training centres, and research establishments then we can say that their main intent is to foster the cultural, intellectual and spiritual life of the community. Their task is not to make a product with maximum efficiency nor to provide a uniform service like a bus company or a restaurant.

How then can such institutions maximize their creative work? One answer is to suggest forms of organisation which support, encourage and develop the free creative powers of the teacher, the priest, the architect or the scientist. It is after all the individual human being who out of his or her spiritual and intellectual capacities is able to generate the ideas and insights needed by others and society. This means that organisational forms which support the freedom of the professional are most appropriate.

In today's society this is frequently not the case, as the lessons of management science usually gained in the field of industrial consultancy are applied indiscriminately to all types of institutions. In many colleges, schools and research institutions an out of date 'industrial model' of organisation is applied. The result is that administrators regard themselves as managers and teachers and researchers as workers, with support staff feeling that they are not seen at all. The consequence of such an approach is that both professional staff and support staff organize themselves into unions and feel that they are the serfs of the system. As they rightly argue, efficiency and numbers seems to be the only thing that counts, education suffers and bitterness abounds.[7]

For cultural initiatives a professional, collegial model is best suited. This means that professionals form collegial bodies in which the central aims and policies of the institutions are discussed and decided upon, leaving the teachers a high degree of autonomy in the classroom. Administrative functions such as accounting, enrolment, registration, building maintenance and the like are support services, there to support the free creative activity of the teacher or researcher, not to dominate it.

A service institution such as a department of transportation, a restaurant, the welfare office or a hospital has different priorities. It exists to supply uniformity of service to everyone. As such it needs to have clearly understood policies and procedures which are followed by everyone. Unique solutions and new ideas do not add much to the processing of a motor vehicle registration except confusion. While the Kafkaesque quality of bureaucracies are well known, service institutions quite rightly have a rule and procedure orientation. For them, organising in work groups which understand, follow and administer the service process is essential. The processing of baggage and passengers in an airport or of a meal order in a restaurant asks for small work groups who understand their tasks and the customers' needs so that customers are responded to in an efficient and courteous manner. The heart of these institutions is the service team just as the heart of the cultural institution is the creative professional. Peoples Airlines has understood this and asks all its employees, including top and middle management to spend some time every year as flight attendants and counter personnel.[8]

Product institutions again have a different central mission – that of producing maximum quantity and quality at minimum cost. Efficiency is paramount – planning, doing and controlling efficient work processes so that minimum error and wastage results. While this aim led to highly structured, specialised, hierarchical organisations in the mass production industries the shift toward more technologically sophisticated production and greater variation in product has encouraged the creation of flexible product and project teams.[9] Decentralised, flatter organisations with well trained production teams are emerging in more and more industries as computerisation allows greater mechanisation and sharing of cost and production information.

Product organisations serve our bodily needs using nature's wealth and human ingenuity. They require high levels of specialisation and manifest an extensive degree of inter-dependence between work processes such as procurement, planning, marketing, production, quality control and shipping. The heart of the product organisation is the production team.

If we compare this typology of institutions to the image of the human being previously discussed then it can be observed that each type of institution has a primary relationship to one aspect of the human being. Cultural institutions both serve the individual human spirit and require the psychological and spiritual creativity of the individual teacher, researcher and artist if they are to function well. Service institutions exist to provide a uniform, equal service to all human beings – they in a sense serve the soul and body needs of each of us – treating us equally as fellow sojourners on earth. Product institutions mainly serve our bodily needs – having to deal with the material laws of scarcity in producing quality goods efficiently.

The relevant distinctions between the different types of institutions can be summarised as follows:

I. *Cultural Institutions* – Colleges, schools, research institutions, architect offices, lawyers, professional associations.

Central Aims: Providing unique insights, ideas, answers, education to individuals and groups.

Organisational Form: Collegial association of professionals supported by administrative and clerical services.

Needs Served: Intellectual and spiritual needs of individuals and communities.

Dominant Principle: Individual creativity and freedom of the professional.

II. *Service Institutions* – Public bureaucracies, transport services, welfare offices, hospitals, restaurants and other service institutions.

Central Aims: Uniform service to all customers.

Organisational Form: Flexible service teams capable of understanding and responding to customer needs efficiently and courteously.

Needs Served: Soul and physical needs of individuals and groups.

Dominant Principle: Equality of customers.

III. *Product Institutions* – Car and steel manufacturers, toymakers, food processors, glass manufacturers and other production orientated companies.

Central Aims: Efficiency of production; maximising quality and quantity at minimum cost.

Organisational Form: Flexible, skilled interdependent production teams.

Needs Served: Physical and soul needs of customers and the community.

Dominant Principle: Specialisation, efficiency and interdependence of work teams.

As in all typologies, this description highlights the differences between institutions and plays down the similarities. Of course an institution, such as a college, has significant features of a service and a product organisation; for example the processing of student applications, the maintenance of a cafeteria and the running of a press. The same is true of a service institution or a company. Each contains aspects of all three types of institutional forms. What is however crucial is that the central organisational aim is not lost sight of so that an out of date industrial model does not produce a societal landscape consisting entirely of product institutions in which financial return is the only yardstick of excellence. In our experience this danger is particularly pronounced in school and college systems largely funded by the state with numerical funding systems. College and school administrators are then chosen for their financial know-how and political connections, not their understanding of education.

In what way is such a typology relevant to a discussion of new initiatives and new social forms? First, it suggests the direction in which appropriate aims for different types of new initiatives can be located. A new school or a counselling centre is not a product institution and a new shoe factory is not a service institution. While this appears obvious it is surprising how often such distinctions are overlooked and meaningful goals are neglected in favour of production goals and profitability. More importantly such a typology suggests that organisational principles and forms vary according to different goals and that new initiatives will be more likely to prosper if they focus on those forms most likely to enhance their central 'product' or 'service'.

If we return to the question of new social forms and individual consciousness raised at the beginning of this chapter, then it becomes quite clear that the more the individual worker or professional is given the opportunity of understanding and contributing to the goals of the initiative, the more he or she is able to function in a manner consistent with the interests of the initiative as a whole. The clearer and the more shared the central vision is, the more the individual and the service or production group can be given responsibility. In new initiatives this possibility is greater than in those institutions where departmental egotism or labour management conflicts are already well entrenched. Yet even in older institutions it is surprising what activity and enthusiasm can be generated at all levels of the organisation if people are given the opportunity of participating in developing a vision of the future and in taking steps to realise those goals. A large factory of Ford in Germany entered such a process with initial reluctance and then generated ideas and activities of many kinds from supervisory level to top management.[10] A college in Ontario suffering from conflicts between the faculty and the Administration developed a joint image of the future despite initial fears and found that they saw the same reality and wished to pursue common goals.

Understanding and participating in meaningful goal setting and taking up responsibilities for the totality is not only important for organisational renewal but is also an essential step in helping individuals move out of a 'me first and only' orientation.

Chapter Four

Ways of Working Together

Tijno Voors and Christopher Schaefer

Meeting Forms

Three realms of organisational life and three types of initiatives have been described in chapter three. What implications does this view of initiatives have for the forms of working together in meetings?

When an initiative starts, a small carrying group tends to make many decisions quickly and informally. In starting a school, a small parent group will meet periodically over supper and decide issues of hiring, name, and location in a series of quick conversations. A new store in Montreal received its beginning and initial impetus from discussions between a young couple who grabbed whatever time was available to work out the myriad decisions needed for a new enterprise. However, even in this exciting childhood period of initiatives, it is important for initiative-takers to draw distinctions between different types of issues and to, whenever possible, create meetings which primarily address one area of decision-making so that a hodge-podge of issues does not produce excessive tiredness and irritation.

We saw that organisations, like individuals, have an identity which comes to expression in the central goals of the initiative, in its philosophy, name, approach to customers and in its advertising material. The small store in Montreal became La Futonerie and was dedicated to the manufacture and sale of high quality, custom made, natural fibre Futons (bedding). The school became the Lexington Waldorf School based on the principles of Waldorf education. Initiative-takers need to create special meetings in which such questions of identity can be discussed, in which the vision of the initiative and the needs of customers and clients can be explored.

Such meetings in which the spiritual impulse of the initiative is nurtured can best be organised a few times a year as work days or as *conference meetings* involving everyone connected with the initiative.

A different type of meeting which needs to take place more frequently, once a week or at least twice a month, is the *co-workers meeting*. Here the soul and social dimension of the initiative is discussed. Questions of hiring, work conditions, salary questions, task divisions will be debated and decided upon by the carrying group.

Meetings devoted to the everyday work of the initiative again have a different quality. Tasks need to be coordinated on a daily and a weekly basis; the ordering of supplies, the review of accounts, and the checking of orders needs to take place. While such meetings will differ in content between a school, a restaurant and a small manufacturing plant they are highly specific in nature, and involve those who are directly involved in specific tasks.

The first kind of meeting in essence involves a dialogue with the spirit of the initiative, the second a dialogue between co-workers and the third a dialogue with the earth – with money, resources and administrative questions.

Even in the beginning years of the initiative these distinctions are important to keep in mind so that there can be an adequate focus and time for each area of organisational life.

The Conference: Working on Identity Questions

The Conference or Work Days have the function of allowing reflection on the essential questions facing initiatives. Such a meeting, lasting a number of days, allows a review of the past, a surfacing of present issues and a re-dedication to a common future. Whether the initiative is new or already well-established such a review of the past and a discussion of the future is vital to the institution's health. It is like our own need as individuals to occasionally step back from the pressures of everyday life in order to see what is essential in our lives and what new directions are called for.

It is important that such meetings or conferences develop a rhythm, a regularity in the course of the year. Strength is built on repetition. For many of the initiatives we have worked with an annual or semi-annual conference or retreat was the only opportunity individuals had to explore basic questions and equally vital, to get to know each other better as people. Such meetings should be open to all who are involved in the initiative. In the case of a school it should involve teachers, board members, administrative staff and parents who have demonstrated an on-going commitment to the school by serving on committees or carrying out other school responsibilities. Other institutions such as counselling or therapy centres, consultancy organisations or architects find such workdays can involve not only professional staff but also support staff, advisory board members, and occasionally family members and valued clients. The same holds true of smaller service organisations and companies.

In arranging such meetings it is often good to leave the usual workplace and find an inexpensive retreat centre, a farm or some other location in which individuals can relax while reviewing the central questions of their work life.

Since in most cases such conferences or retreats cover one or more days, a balance of activities should be sought. In our work with clients, we recommend some artistic activity in the morning after breakfast (singing, movement, sculpture, painting), followed either by a common study or a talk by an outside person knowledgeable about a field which is of interest to the initiative or a prepared talk by someone in the carrying group. Then there can be time for discussing some of the central questions which the initiative faces; for example:

> Why did enrolment decrease in our school last year? How can we improve teacher/parent relationships? Why is our consultancy company only attracting service or cultural institutions as clients? How can we become more visible in our community as a whole food cafe? Why is there a lack of commitment in our organisation? How can we improve our meetings and improve the mood among staff? Can we develop a renewed image of the future which articulates our values and priorities?

The discussion of such questions is best held in groups of twelve or less so that individuals have the opportunity to speak and to be heard. Such a division into groups, however, then requires a common sharing in the whole circle.

Then comes lunch and perhaps a digestive walk or some physical work. It is surprising how conducive repair work, raking leaves or gardening can be for heart to heart talks. Further discussion in groups can take place in the afternoon, followed by an enjoyable supper. The evening is best spent in social activity, music or story telling or reading. Occasionally an inspirational talk for everyone can also serve to energize reflection and encourage sleep.

Work days or a conference meeting is less to make practical decisions than to form a picture of present issues and future possibilities and to help enliven a vision of the initiative and its mission in the world. Issues will need further discussion and decision in project groups or committees.

Periodic conference or retreat meetings of this type are vital to the health of all types of institutions, because they contribute to regeneration and development.

Levels of Listening – Helps and Hindrances

To be effective listeners, we must learn to listen to the whole person – not just to the words he/she is saying, but also to what lies between or behind the actual words.

We need to listen to *thoughts*, to *feelings*, and to *intentions*.

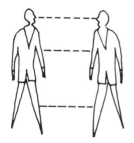

'Head listening'
to facts, concepts, arguments, ideas.

'Heart listening'
to emotions, values, mood, experience.

'Listening for the will'
energy, direction, motivation.

The Thinking Level

The most obvious way to listen – apparently 'objective' – but not as effective as we imagine. Can we truly follow with our own thoughts, the thoughts of the speaker? We think much faster than he/she speaks – how do we use this extra mental time – to synthesise and digest what we are hearing, or to think our own separate thoughts?

Hindrances on this level include problems of attention and accuracy, but also arise from the different *frames of reference* held by speaker and listener. Our knowledge, concepts, vocabulary and way of thinking derive from the *past* – our own

Continued

individual past education and experience. If we do not allow for the fact that the other person has his own, perhaps very different, frame of reference, it is all too easy to get our wires crossed, or to assume a level of understanding which is not real. We continually run the danger of over-complicating or over-simplifying what we hear.

The listening process is *supported* on this level by the cultivation of a genuine *interest* in 'where the other person is coming from' – an open-minded approach which does not judge *his/her* words according to *my* preconceptions.

The Feeling Level

Listening on this level means penetrating a step deeper into the other's experience – apparently rational statements may be covering feelings of distress, anger, embarrassment etc. These may be heard more through the tone of voice, facial expression, gesture, etc, than is what is actually said, and can be obscured, especially if we are unaccustomed to, or inhibited about, expressing feelings directly.

Accurate perception of feelings is continually *impaired* by the effects of our *own* feelings, the likes and dislikes which arise in us semi-consciously in the face of certain people, situations or issues. Even the mention of certain 'trigger' words or phrases can call up quite strong emotions in us, which obscure our perception of what the *other* is feeling.

Continued

Effective listening can be *fostered* on the feeling level by 'quietening our own reactions to the immediate impressions we receive, and developing the quality of *empathy*. This means allowing ourselves calmly to 'live into' the other person's experience as he/she is speaking. The faculty of *social sensibility* which can be trained in this way is a key attribute of skilled negotiators.

The Will Level

To sense the real intentions of another person can be one of the hardest aspects of the art of listening. Often, speakers are themselves only dimly aware of what they actually *want* in a situation. Skilful listening can help to discover, 'behind' the thoughts and 'below' the feelings involved, the real sources of potential energy and commitment. This will often involve sensing what is left unsaid. The *future* lies asleep in people's will-forces.

One impulse of the will which is only too quick to awaken is the urge towards power and conflict, to impose my own will and resist the other person's. Resistance at the level of intention is often *rational-ised* into arguments which can never be resolved, because the basic *will* to reach agreement is not present. If I allow these adversarial forces to arise in me whilst listening, I create an immediate barrier to a creative future work-relationship.

If I can hold back 'my way' of acting in the situation, and continually look for elements of common direction and mutuality, I may be able to open the way towards future co-operation.

Ineffective Listening

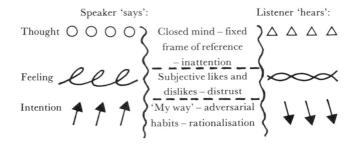

Effective Listening

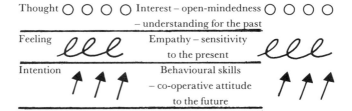

Active effective listening on these three levels will be a substantial, creative contribution in many realms of social and professional life.

Continued

Exercise – Listening on Three Levels

Aim: To practise skills of listening in the following ways:

1. Accuracy and attention in relation to the information, ideas and mental pictures actually expressed by the speaker.

2. Sensitivity to the underlying feelings and mood, which may or may not be directly expressed.

3. Recognising the fundamental direction of the speaker's intentions and energy.

Method:

Groups of 4. One person relates a recent experience which contains a certain problem or question for him/her, which is still open or unresolved. Each listener takes one level.

After the speaker has finished and a brief pause for reflection, the listeners are asked to share their observations in the following ways respectively:

1. Re-tell in your own words the main elements of the story you heard. What facts and concepts did the speaker use to make that situation clear?

2. Describe the feelings you imagine were present

Continued

in the speaker:
> a) in the past situation which was described.
> b) during the telling.

3. What kinds of motivation could you perceive in the speaker? What does/did he/she want to *do* about the situation described? How much commitment and energy is present, and in what directions?

All observations are then checked with the story-teller. How accurate was the listening? What was missed? Did the feedback make the speaker more aware of certain semi-conscious factors? Distinguish between observation and interpretation – how justified was the latter?

Repeat with new tellers – possible also with listeners all taking all levels, building up feedback together on each.

The Carrying Group Meetings

The co-workers who are able and willing to carry responsibility for the whole of the initiative should meet regularly. This meeting focuses on the aims of the initiative, on coordination of tasks and on organisational and policy questions. This group will, for example, have to develop and review the approach to customers, to new products, and to publicity. They will need to discuss personnel questions and policies of salaries for part-time and full-time workers and questions of tuition or price. They will also regularly look at central tasks and the division of responsibilities. It is advisable to have these meetings fairly regularly, perhaps once a week. In new initiatives the question of who should be part of these meetings arises. The answer is those who both feel responsible and have demonstrated their commitment to the initiatives and its aims. Being there at least a year or more is vital so that one understands the culture, mood and work life of the institution.

The nature and atmosphere of the carrying group meeting is different from that of the conference. One will always experience the pressure of time in these meetings. The agenda is often long and a lot of information is exchanged that needs to be weighed and judged. Sometimes quite different points of view have to be brought together and strong differences of opinion will arise. In the carrying group meetings, one exercises the *art of balance,* of give and take, of breathing together. The secret, the heart of the meeting lies in the fact that everyone can speak, that everyone can experience being heard and that a sense of mutual equality and dedication arises. This of course takes time and a process of joint learning. A careful preparation of meetings, an agreed upon process of decision-making and a review of meetings is essential.

The agenda of the meeting needs to be clear to members of the group before-hand so that an inner preparation is possible. We have all experienced the dilemma of arriving at meetings, breathless from our last task, with not a clue about what is going to be discussed. So everyone needs to have some idea of what is coming toward them, preferably in the form of a brief agenda noting the issues to be discussed and something of their relative priority. New issues can of course be added as the agenda is reviewed at the beginning of the meeting.

For the carrying group short minutes are also important so that issues discussed, decided upon and delegated to someone for implementation can be reviewed. Without such minutes it is easy to forget what was agreed to and even easier to forget what you were supposed to do between one meeting and the next.

Approaches to decision-making and suggestions for the

review of meetings will be discussed later in this chapter.

Work Meetings

The third kind of meeting to be held regularly is the work meeting. The daily work must be done with care. Activities must be co-ordinated and work processes planned. Supplies, materials and other resources need to be available at the right moment. The bookkeeping, payment of bills, salaries, and monthly financial reviews must be carried out. In every initiative and organisation the need to divide tasks among smaller work teams or individuals is readily apparent. In schools there are questions of admissions, parent interviews, publicity, scheduling, bookkeeping, maintenance and the ordering of supplies. In smaller production facilities, the needs of marketing, sales, ordering, shipment, production, quality control and accounting are readily apparent and need the attention of one or more individuals.

In dividing work tasks, areas of responsibility need to be clearly defined and reviewed. Often short daily meetings are necessary to inform each other, to coordinate, and to plan and review the work. When the initiative grows, an administrative group will meet regularly and the work meetings will take place within the different sections or work teams.

In work meetings, decisions about work activities need to be made quickly and on the spot. Delegation must be cultivated so that individuals are free to act in their areas of responsibility. It is in the realm of the deed that our work interdependence and co-responsibility become readily apparent. If the food is not ordered for the café the cook cannot function and if a teacher is in a bad mood and poorly prepared on a given day the other teachers will experience the consequences in later lessons.

For many of us being truly responsible is difficult, especially when we are functioning as equals in a new initiative. It is clearer, and of course more compelling if we have a boss. Yet the opportunity for exercising free responsibility, recognizing our interdependence and developing mutual trust is one of the challenges of working collegially, a challenge which will stretch us inwardly and help us develop new social faculties.

There will of course be other kinds of committees and project groups which initiatives will need but the conference, the carrying group and work teams represent the three basic joint activities required of any initiative. Without such a dialogue of the head, the heart and the hand neither the individual nor the institution can work freely and effectively. While all three types of meetings are important for the different types of initiatives, the work or task group meeting is more central for product organisations, the carrying group or policy and procedure meeting for service institutions and the conference or identity meeting for cultural initiatives.

The Mandate Organisation

As an initiative grows in size the initial carrying group or the co-workers meeting has increased difficulties in dealing with the many issues requiring decision and action. Delegation and a differentiation of tasks is required to help the initiative to continue to prosper.

At this point two obstacles appear. One is a democratic tendency in which it is maintained that we have to decide everything together. The result is endless meetings, long agendas and much discussion without much action. In some schools in which we have worked the collegium or co-workers meeting regularly had twenty to twenty-five items to discuss in a single meeting including disciplinary action against an individual child, Christmas fair publicity, class trip questions, financial requests for conference attendance and how to look for a new French teacher. Many of these issues should be worked on by individuals and small committees yet everyone wants to feel involved. The other obstacle is an autocratic or oligarchic tendency in which one or two work-horses do most of the work and wield the power behind the scenes. Neither tendency is healthy for the initiative, hiding the real need to establish a 'republican' mandate structure in which the variety of tasks necessary for the running of the school, the shop, or the therapeutic centre is clearly delegated or mandated to individuals or small groups. This implies that an individual or a committee is given the mandate to make decisions on behalf of the whole organisation in clearly defined areas of work.

The creation of a mandate system in an organisation above all requires clarity and trust. Clarity through having a shared vision of the aims and purposes of the organisation, and also clarity about its policies, and decision-making procedures. This means that the conference on the workdays are vital as an ongoing part of the initiative's life – in order to renew the shared vision. It also suggests a transformation of the co-workers meeting from the space in which all important decisions are decided to the space in which mainly policies are made and mandates allocated. Policies are guiding principles – such as what kind of co-workers are we looking for, what is our salary system or policy, what guidelines do we have on scholarships, and what image and qualities do we wish to project in our fairs and publicity material. If there are clear policies in the areas of pricing, personnel, research, publicity, and the like, then an individual or a committee is capable of making decisions for the whole.

In establishing a mandate system the initiative and the mandate holders need to be aware of the following principles:

- The area of responsibility must be clearly defined by the carrying group meeting, and regularly reviewed.
- The mandate holder (or committee) is autonomous in taking decisions within their designated mandate area.
- The mandates are held for a limited period of time, usually for 1 or 2 years, and a maximum of

3 years.
- Mandate holders may take a specific decision to the carrying group meeting in case of uncertainty or gravity of consequence. This does not mean that they are giving up their mandate.
- Carrying group meetings need to take place regularly to enable mandate holders to listen carefully to the information, ideas, opinions, and feelings that are expressed and to clarify policy questions.

An understanding and mutual listening between the committees and the carrying group meeting is a pre-condition for the maintenance of trust in the organisation. The mandate holders take decisions which often influence the work situations of their colleagues. The basis for a willingness to accept and execute decisions of a committee or a mandate holder lies in the mutual acceptance of the mandate principles, and the daily experience that the trust given to the mandate holder is used in a healthy way. The readiness with which co-workers accept decisions – even when one has a differing opinion about the specific situation – is an essential aspect of a collegial way of working. In this sense mandating means learning to accept the other's specific talents, their one-sidedness, and their judgements. Through a mandate structure one practices mutual acceptance and collegiality as well as creating a more efficient work organisation.

One of the most delicate aspects of creating a delegation system based on clear mandates is the question of the selection and appointment of mandate holders. One way of approaching this issue is through the principle of co-option. The committee or the individual mandate holder thereby accepts the task of finding a successor or successors. If this way is chosen by the initiative then the following procedures are helpful:

1) The mandate holders decide to transfer or pass

on their specific mandate to a new group.

2) The functioning of the mandate or of the committee is reviewed by the co-workers, collegium or policy-making body and the mandate tasks are again discussed.

3) The mandate holders look for successors who they feel possess the capability of carrying out the designated tasks efficiently and well.

4) The suggested names are mentioned in the carrying group meeting and an open conversation takes place with the suggested members of the new committee as well as of the old. Out of this conversation it can be seen whether the new group has the confidence of the co-workers or whether a different individual or individuals are required.

5) The new mandate holders are then appointed by the old.

In this way a new publicity committee, a financial planning group or a parent contact person can be selected for a school.

A modification of the co-option principle is for the carrying group meeting to select new mandate holders on the basis of the recommendation of the previous group. However, what is important, is not to fall into the trap of volunteerism. Some schools and educational institutions delegate tasks mainly on the basis of who is willing to do the job. This can result in the less capable people doing a task. It is after all very difficult to say 'no' to someone in a volunteer system. For work to be done well competence is required. Unfortunately we are not yet very able to judge our own levels of skill and competence and need the help of colleagues in seeing our strengths and weaknesses.

In any mandate structure it is important to set clear time limits to a certain group carrying out the mandate and equally to let them carry it out without interference. Except in cases of gross negligence the mandate should not be recalled or terminated except at the request of the mandate holders.

As an initiative develops and begins to delegate or mandate tasks the question of who should be on the policy-making body or the carrying group meeting arises. Initially everyone, part and full-time people, may have been part of the initiative group. But now the need for continuity and commitment becomes important, for the carrying group is the heart and the guiding organ of the initiative. It is this group, often referred to as a College of Teachers in Waldorf Schools which needs the insight and strength to understand the totality of the initiative, to nurture it and to guide it into the future.

We have looked at three basic meetings in an initiative; the Conference connected to goals, to the mission of the organisation, the carrying group meeting for developing the guiding principles and policies, of colleagueship, and the work meetings for carrying out specific tasks. This division gives one an insight into criteria for membership in the co-workers group, collegium or policy-making body. In our experience three types of questions are important to discuss with a potential new member of the carrying group:

1) Do they inwardly share the goals and philosophy of the organisation? In other words do they feel connected to the mission of the organisation? (Spiritual Community)

2) Do they feel humanly connected to their colleagues? Are they perceived as fitting into the 'social community' of the initiative? (Social Community)

3) Do they manifest sufficient professional competence to be part of the permanent work community? (Work Community)*

*See Chapter One

It is usually best to make such criteria visible to potential members of the co-workers group or collegium and to allow the individual to request membership after one or more years in the organisation. Once they have requested they can address these questions in the full circle of colleagues and be asked questions by the others. After such a discussion the existing co-worker group can then decide whether membership is appropriate for the person in question.

It is best not to keep criteria for membership hidden and to select some people and not others based on a process that is invisible to the faculty as a whole. In some Waldorf schools membership on the collegium is experienced as a highly political and hidden process in which favoritism abounds. Clarity of procedure and criteria of membership avoids unnecessary speculation and ill will.

In developing a mandate organisation it becomes important to have a *co-ordinating group* which plans the co-workers meeting and co-ordinates activities within the initiative. This group needs to be well informed about the different mandate areas. Its co-ordination function is of central importance for the nurturing of good communication, and must be seen as a separate mandate. The co-ordination group is not the executive of the initiative but rather a facilitating, communication and planning organ.

A further condition for a proper functioning of the mandate structure is a salary arrangement that is in agreement with the collegiate model described. No financial consequences are attached to the execution of mandate functions. The mandate structure should be seen as a situational, ever-moving form of working together. In other words: a leadership that, according to the situation, can change. If the execution of a mandate was connected with an increase in salary, improper elements would enter the process of selection, and withdrawal from mandates.

A good example of a mandate organisation is ARTA in Holland. ARTA is a therapeutic centre in Holland, where people suffering from drug addiction can be helped. In 1980, this initiative with 15 co-workers chose to change its hierarchical structures to a new republican structure, in which decision making was mandated to one or more co-workers. They formed a carrying group of co-workers and created the following mandate areas:

- *Admission mandate.* This mandate holder was responsible for developing the admission policy of future residents and became responsible for its implementation.

- *Personnel mandate.* This mandate group, generally responsible for selection, acceptance, and dismissal of co-workers, was specially responsible for the description of the different work functions of the co-workers and the individual development questions of the co-workers.

- *Financial mandate.* This mandate holder was responsible for developing a more conscious relation to money among the co-workers.

- *Therapy mandate.* This mandate group was responsible for all therapeutic aspects of the ARTA programme.

ARTA also has mandates for maintenance, timetabling, external relations, after care, and the very important mandate responsibility of guiding and co-ordinating development of this new structure of decision-making.

Next to the mandates for aspects of the organisation that embrace more than one function, everyone in ARTA has responsibility for his or her own function. In ARTA there are craftsmen or specialists responsible for the professional running of the work areas, finance, administration, garden, kitchen, wood workshop, weavery, and so on. There are also team members and personal counsellors. A doctor, a psychiatrist, and many different art therapists have a part-time relation to ARTA, but have no specific responsibility in the organisation.

Many Waldorf schools and other educational and volunteer organisations have a well developed committee structure which can be transformed into a mandate system by a more conscious articulation of mandates. This involves achieving greater clarity about policies and procedures by the co-workers meeting followed by a common definition of mandate tasks. Such a step is advisable for many of the organisations we work with so that a co-ordination of tasks takes place and so that the many issues of trust among colleagues can be ameliorated through a conscious set of organisational principles and procedures.

In this chapter we have not discussed the question of Boards of directors or other legal questions largely because of the differences in legal codes between different English speaking countries. In both U.S. and Canadian schools, for example, some mandates, or committees will be connected to the board, for example finance, building and grounds and perhaps publicity. The mandating principles are important, whether the mandating group is the college of teachers, the co-workers meeting or a board of directors.

Working Together in Groups

Working together in groups has the same intimate relation to the image of the human being as organisational forms. One can, for example, distinguish between three fundamental types of groups. There are *study groups* whose aim is to help the individual members arrive at a more complete understanding of a text or subject; *social groups* whose aim is to work on human relationships and *work groups,* which are task directed.[1] The first primarily focuses on our thought capacities, the second on our feeling life, while the third calls upon our will.

While this section will deal primarily with work groups, it is important to recognise that the dynamics of all groups are characterised by elements connected to the three soul capacities of the human being. We exchange ideas, concepts and information through words. This content level of group life is strongly connected to our thought life. In addition there is the quality of relationships, the weaving of sympathies and antipathies between group members. This level of feelings is often less visible than the content level but is no less important. I may not agree with another person's idea simply because he or she cut me off less than five minutes ago. Thirdly there is the will life of the group, the common aims and procedures which we follow or don't follow during our discussions.[2]

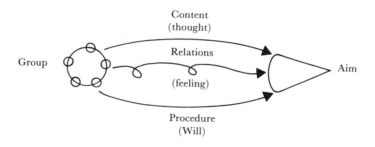

Most working groups are relatively conscious of content, less conscious of relationships and least conscious of procedure. Yet this last area is one of the most essential for initiatives if they are to make effective use of their time and to arrive at collegial decisions. All too often the procedural aspect of group life is neglected with the result that there is limited clarity about the group's aims, its agenda and its process of decision-making.

In focusing on procedure the first essential ingredient for a fruitful meeting is planning. Has the agenda been prepared and sent out to members? Are the aims of the discussion clear? Which issues need decisions and which analysis? What information will be required? How much time should be allocated to each topic?

These questions can be briefly reviewed and discussed at the start of the meeting and new items added to the agenda if deemed necessary. An important distinction to be aware of in the planning phase of the discussion is the difference between problem solving and decision-making. For example the question of how the grading policy in the high school is working is a problem solving question. It is past directed and involves investigation and analysis. The question of what kind of new grading policy should be adopted is a decision-making question directed toward the future and involves the exploration of alternative options.

Typically the planning phase of a meeting is followed by some information sharing, by judging and weighing and then arriving at a conclusion or a decision.

Planning

What agenda items?
How much time?
Aims of the discussion? (decisions –
conclusions, sharing).
Sequence of items and discussion?

Problem Solving (Past Directed)

Decision-Making (Future Directed)

Information-Sharing –
What is our grading policy?
What are our profit margins or losses?

Information-Sharing –
What alternative grading policies or pricing structures are possible?

| When did the child leave the school and why? | What are the ways in which we can avoid losing children from the school unnecessarily? |

(Light of thinking – information)

Judging – Weighing –
What are the most relevant facts in this situation?
Why is the grading policy inadequate?
According to what values and criteria are we judging?

Judging – Weighing –
What are the consequences of the different alternatives?
What principles make one more preferable than the other?

(Feelings – Values)

Conclusion –
Our present grading policy is inadequate.
Our profit margins are too low.
The child was not handled properly (or she was handled adequately by her teacher).

Decision –
We will only begin giving letter grades in tenth grade.
All cosmetic products need a profit margin of 90% before being sold to distributors.
All grave disciplinary cases will be reviewed by a committee before a child is dismissed.

(Will – Conclusions – Decisions)

Review of Meeting

If a group, over time, learns to work creatively with a common procedure such as the one described, then collegial decisions will be much easier. However, too much emphasis on procedure kills the life of the meeting so a sense of balance between procedural consciousness and lively engagement needs cultivation. Generally speaking the larger the group the more form and consciousness is required to produce a fruitful outcome.

The chairperson carries a primary responsibility for seeing that a reasonable procedure is adhered to in a meeting. He or she will also need to guide the interaction – the rhythm of speaking and listening so that confusion, sub-conversations or repeated interruptions can be avoided.

The more mature and developed a group is, the less leadership will be required by a chairperson. However, such development only occurs if a periodic review of the meeting takes place so that a collective awareness of both procedural and interaction patterns can be born. Adults learn most effectively through reflecting on experience. A review or evaluation of group process is an essential tool in bringing about a heightened awareness of what goes on in groups and how the process of working together can be improved. Short evaluations can be held after each co-workers meeting or for a longer time on a periodic basis, for example every third or fourth meeting. Types of questions to be explored include:

Content –   Were our contributions to the point? How was the balance between information and ideas or concepts? Did we discuss the subject(s) adequately?

Interaction – How was the balance between speaking and listening? Did contributions build on each other? Did individuals feel cut off by others? How was the mood of the discussion? How can we improve our listening? How did the chairperson function?

Procedure – Was our agenda clear? Did we achieve our aims? How was our time awareness? Was the judgement process dealt with satisfactorily? How was the sequence of problem solving and decision-making? Have past decisions been carried out?

Questions such as these stimulate reflection and awareness. A group may appoint an observer to help guide the review process but it is important that the group itself reviews rather than that the observer pronounces judgements. It is also important to keep in mind that as much can be learned from what went well as from what didn't.

An additional benefit of evaluation is that it can help the group to build loyalty. After any meeting a review takes place but in the corridors or on the way home. Sitting with friends we tend to give vent to our feelings. An opportunity to do this responsibly in the full circle will over time give a new substance to the meetings as well as decrease the tendency toward irresponsible gossip.

Conclusion

In this chapter we have indicated some principles for working together in initiatives and given suggestions for creating collegial forms. Central to our perspective is the idea that initiatives are human creations based on an image of the human being. By making such an image explicit we have tried to show how a threefold picture of man can both illuminate and give form to ways of working together collegially in our time. All initiatives are involved in a dialogue with the spirit (aim, values, vision) with the human soul world (customers, clients, co-workers) and with the earth (buildings, machines, resources). Developing and maintaining these dialogues is one pre-condition of organisational health. The other is finding those forms capable of enhancing the creativity, dedication, enthusiasm and social responsibility of ourselves as co-workers and colleagues.

Group – Problem Solving Procedure

A. Sorting Out The Question
Clarifying The Problem

I PLANNING

'Warmth'	What do we hope to achieve?
	What is our aim?
	Are we the right people?
	How are we going to go about it?
	Do we need a chairman?
	What will he do for us?
	Do we need a scribe?...a timekeeper?
	How much time have we got?
	How best to use it?
	What facilities do we need?
	Flipcharts? Blackboard?

II BUILDING A COMMON PICTURE

'Light'	Gather information
	Members' experiences – examples – views of the problem

III WEIGHING, FORMING JUDGEMENTS

'Movement'   Sort out important factors
(CRITERIA)
Values to be taken into
account

IV DRAWING CONCLUSION

'Form'   Bring out a common understanding of the problem.

*B. Solving The Problem
Deciding Which Action To Take*

I 2ND PLANNING STAGE

'Warmth'   Are we certain we share the
same aims?
What are our objectives?

II EXPLORE ALTERNATIVE OPTIONS

'Light'   Identify possible solutions.
Examine their consequences.

III WEIGH UP

'Movement'   What is the effect of possible
consequences on individual
members?
How do they feel about them?
Watch for common view
emerging.
Criteria for choice?

IV DECIDE AND AGREE ACTION

'Form'   What needs to be done?
What do we want to do?

Organise who will do what.
Agree a procedure to monitor
progress.

REVIEW

How have we got on?
Have we achieved our
objectives?
What can we learn from the
experience?
Have we listened to each
other?
Is anyone frustrated?
Are we going to carry
through our action plan?
How do we feel?
Are we moving towards be-
coming a mature group?
Do we need to meet again as
a group?

Chapter Five

Funding Initiatives

Stephen Briault & Warren Ashe

1. Money as Problem and Challenge

Every new project wishing to find its place in social life, will meet the necessity of obtaining and effectively handling finance. In some cases this challenge will be met from the outset; in other projects, especially where the aims are primarily social and cultural rather than economic, there may be a certain reluctance to enter consciously in this realm. Quite often financial responsibility devolves onto one or two individuals in the initiative. This isolation can become a considerable burden for such people; it can also become an apparent or real source of power within the project. Many institutions striving to bring something new and worthwhile into social life, show a constant struggle and insecurity in the financial realm, and this can undermine great human efforts and sacrifices.

To overcome these dangers, ways of understanding and handling money will need to be developed, which can be accessible to all those involved, so as to free the carriers of the initiative from the paralysis and feelings of helplessness which often surround this field. Working with finances must be seen as an integral part of the initiative-process; through money a project finds and sustains its earthly 'body' in social life. The financial profile of an organisation expresses in abstract form how far and in what way the initiative has been able to 'find its feet'.

This chapter will offer some perspectives on the way in which money moves and acts in social life and in organisations, and derive from these perspectives a number of principles for the management of the capital and the revenue aspects of financing initiatives. It will also describe a range of experiences gained through trying to work in new ways with money, and introduce the aims and methods of Mercury Provident Society, itself a significant new initiative in the field of banking.

2. The Threefold Nature of Social Life and of Finance

The initiators of any enterprise need to use wealth to bring it to life. This applies to a garden plot or a research project, a church or a motor manufacturer. If the initiators do not have enough wealth of their own, they will need access to others' wealth. The *social* character of the undertaking will be in part determined by the immediate source and the form of that wealth. However, it is the essential *functional* character of the enterprise that will determine the nature of the wealth needed to launch it.

There are three primal functions or purposes that may be discerned in human enterprises. The first we may term economic. Any undertaking supplying saleable material, goods or services to meet consumer demand is primarily economic. A retail shop, an airline, a structural engineering firm, and a pig farm are all examples of this kind of activity; they are commercial and industrial because their purpose is to serve bodily needs: to make goods accessible, to transport people and goods, to guide and improve the construction of buildings, and to produce food, respectively. Their funding ultimately is to be met from the proceeds of their goods or the charges made for their services. If they are consistently unprofitable, there may be good reason to dismantle them. (The practice of subsidising an economic activity is simply using the profits of other units in the economy to enable unprofitable units to continue, rightly or wrongly). If they are profitable, they may grow or they may benefit financially those who own them or have capitalised them. But in the end their continued existence depends on the *profitable* provision of goods and services to consumers. The exchange taking place in their transactions provides the wealth they depend on.

A second category of human social activities we may call political. The word leaves a bad taste in the mouths of many these days, so it needs some elaboration. By 'political' is meant those areas of action that directly deal with civic equality and rights, i.e. the processes of law-making, of law enforcement and execution, and of jurisprudence. The boundaries of legitimate governmental action are, of course, a matter of intense debate, and need not concern us here. The point is that they apply to every citizen equally, and thus are funded by all equally, in the form of taxes. This is not to say that each citizen pays an equal amount, but that the same criteria of levy apply; no individual may evade payment as a citizen in the way he may refrain from expenditure as a consumer of products in commercial-industrial life. In return, the State is uniformly zealous in guarding the rights of each citizen, rich or poor. There is an implied political contract between the State and the individual, just as there was a social contract amongst peasants, priests and nobility in feudal Europe. (The fact that this contract is so often broken or distorted by both parties does not detract from its validity or from the fact that it is recognised as true by most minds in the world, even though the notion of what constitutes rights is a matter of fundamental disagreement.) The wealth in the form of taxes that changes hands under the political contract does not generate profit.

The third type of intention that may inform human activity is cultural-spiritual. The doctor, the teacher, the pure research scientist, the artist, and the priest are good examples of bearers of the spiritual life. Their work does not concern itself directly with meeting the material needs of people, nor with establishing the laws that guarantee their rights. They occupy themselves with providing spiritual nourishment, with enlightenment, with the exploration of ideas and feelings in their own right. It will be clear that teachers (except those engaged in vocational training) and the therapeutic occupations, in so far as they concern themselves with the total human well-being for its own sake, fit this category. This category of activity does not make any direct economic contribution to society, but must be supported by the economy in the form of gifts. (The fact that in much of the world the State now supports or administers education, medicine, much scientific research and some of the arts, funding them by taxation, does not alter their dependence on the economy; few people would dispute the fact that they are not saleable, if only because they should be freely available.) Cultural-spiritual activity gives to the economic life enhanced human capacities and new insights, but its economic effects are only indirect: if a doctor by his skill enables a worker to be more productive, this does not mean that the doctor is a production worker.

These brief and necessarily incomplete sketches of the three spheres of society – or the three primary colours of human activity – are a necessary framework for thinking about the funding of new enterprises, for the three spheres have their counterparts within each enterprise, and each enterprise functions in all three spheres. The whole reflects the contribution of each part, and each part is a microcosm of the whole. But any enterprise has an *essentially* economic, political or cultural-spiritual character which derives from the purpose for which it is established and run. Thus a new school exists to develop the minds and values of children, a publishing firm to produce and provide books for sale, the government of a nation to codify and enforce the norms of its culture in legislation. This is true even though the school is a consumer of economic goods, the publisher must concern himself with employee's rights (their political status within the company) and the government concerns itself with spiritual-cultural ideas in forming policy.

When the essential functional character of a new enterprise is grasped, the strategies of financing can be developed. For initiators of enterprises to approach this problem more effectively, it is necessary to look at the character of money itself, for the character of the funding should match the character of the enterprise.

Our primary experience of money is as 'cash in hand' or money in one's pocket, and it is usually connected with a transaction, say the buying of goods. This kind of transaction takes place to the mutual advantage – providing the price is just – of both vendor and purchaser; the vendor needs the money more than he needs the goods, and the purchaser needs the goods more than he needs the money. The mutuality, whether or not the participants are aware of it, underlies every deal, and the fluctuation in prices and market conditions can be seen as adjustments to the buyer and seller relationships. The money concerned – the purchasing medium – circulates at the same rate as the production – distribution – consumption cycle moves. We may call money in this aspect *purchase money*.

The purchase money passing into the hands of a producer or a vendor usually includes an element of profit; and the resources of a consumer are not always exhausted by his purchases, for he abstains from some consumption in order to accumulate 'savings'.* This surplus purchase money is

---

*   'Savings' is a serious misnomer; by this term we usually in fact mean investment capital, since people 'save' by putting money with investment institutions such as banks or brokers.

available for other functions. It can become either *loan money* or *gift money*.

Loan money is temporarily surplus to needs; it is placed on loan because its owner sees that it may be required at some future time but can postpone the spending of it. In the case of company profits,* loan money is usually made available until capital expenditure may be necessary. The lender and borrower have a common aim – or at least they bear common responsibility for the consequences of their transaction; if the borrower uses the loan to produce poison gas, the lender is co-responsible for the product, for his help has been indispensible in getting it onto the market.

Gift money has a special character. Unlike purchase money, which is the medium of people seeking mutual advantage, or loan money, which serves to join people in common responsibility, gift money has the effect, if properly handled, of liberating people. Thus a free donation to a church does not oblige the clergy to please the donor in services or sermons; a free donation to a school does not mean that teachers must follow the educational philosophy favoured by the donor. It is frequently the reverse, and rightly so: the donor has confidence in the church or school and follows its lead in matters religious and educational, leaving it free to develop according to its own lights. (This is just the opposite of the producer-consumer relationship where consumer demand determines what is produced.) But it is easier said than done to make a *free* donation, with no strings – not even unexpressed expectations – attached. It happens most frequently in the case of legacies, but even there the legatee may feel constrained to follow the wishes of a benefactor. To give and to receive freely is not an easily acquired attribute.

---

* This is not to say that all profits are of one kind; some may result from the production-distribution-consumption cycle, others from speculation or even dishonesty. Nevertheless, in so far as they are surplus to current needs, these monies are available as loans.

3. *Money for Initiatives – Capital Financing and New Directions in Banking*

The brief rehearsal above of the three types of money – purchase, loan, gift – is worth thinking about for anyone undertaking a new initiative because it really describes three different *relationships*. If an enterprise is financed with one type of money, the relationship between it and its supporters will be quite different from the relationship that would arise if another kind of money were used. This relationship will be an objective economic fact and may have nothing to do with the personal relationships among the individuals concerned. Let it be said, however, that there are but few undertakings that are born out of and successfully exist upon the freedom implicit in true gift money. Purchase and loan money reflect mutual advantage and common aims respectively, and each involves contractual obligations. Freedom, of course, is just the opposite of obligation. The apparently unsecured future and the necessity for constant renewal of the relationship between donor and recipient involve hard work and a sense of inspiration that goes beyond confidence. Do not build on gifts unless you can muster enduring strength.

Let us now look more closely at the statement that, *'the character of the funding should match the essential functional character of the enterprise.'*

An economic initiative concerns itself primarily with the buying and selling of goods or services; when it is first established, it needs capital, and the provider of capital – a bank or an investor – will seek to determine whether the buying and selling will be sufficiently profitable to give a return on the capital (in the form of interest or dividends) and to repay it within the specified term. It is a risk, a venture undertaken jointly by capitaliser and entrepreneur; similarly, profits are shared. It is the customers' purchase money that makes a production or trading enterprise profitable, and the financial skill is to balance costs, prices, capital requirements and efficient working methods to produce profit without offending against human values. No matter how it is achieved, however, the loan is being repaid by the use of purchase money.

A loan to a spiritual-cultural enterprise on the other hand, cannot rely on profitable handling of purchase money for repayment. It will, if the enterprise wishes to function as a *free* entity, have to receive free gifts to repay its original funding. If the surrounding community can give a free undertaking to donate sufficient funds to repay a loan, the same security can be achieved as when managerial expertise and customer satisfaction combine to make a commercial enterprise profitable. Willingness to donate is, however, quite a different thing from the wish to buy, sell and trade, and the ability to inspire and attract gifts is a valuable trait in a spiritual-cultural enterprise. It is not, however, the same as salesmanship. The potential donor can only give *freely* if he recognises in the enterprise and in himself the same spiritual intentions. There must be clarity of awareness as well as warmth of feeling if the giving of funds is to be healthy and reliable. It is all-important, therefore, that those responsible for initiating a school, a church, a youth club or a hospital should be able to express their aims clearly, and that when it begins to function, the initiative is itself an expression of the same impulse.

Whether an enterprise needs gifts, contractual agreements, or purchase money to sustain its activity, initially it is likely to ask for loan money, and thus it may approach a bank or an organisation like the Mercury Provident Society. Mercury was established in order to find a way of handling loan money that would enhance awareness of the nature of such money and the relationships it creates and manifests. As a licensed deposit-taking institution, Mercury tries to act as a lens between depositor (lender) and borrower. Depositors are asked to specify to whom they wish to lend their money; a list of borrowers is published, and the skill of the banker consists in helping to make the right match. An important step in this process, however, is the examination of projects seeking loans. For some, loan money is inappropriate; for others, a loan may create more problems than it solves. In any case, Mercury must look at the project with a view to testing its viability, its social health and its essential character.

The banker must always observe confidentiality, so it is not possible to include here an actual case history, but there are set out below two imaginary case histories amalgamating features of several projects that have come Mercury's way. The details are less important that the central thrust of the investigations, which focus on three areas:

1) The purpose or motive for the existence of the enterprise and the needs that it will serve.

2) The social structure of the undertaking: its legal form and ownership, decision-making processes and relationship to outside supporters.

3) The financial support – capital, guarantees, gifts or customers – that it is able to attract.

Case History One: Henry Smith

The Idea and the People.

Henry Smith came to us with the wish to produce hand-made wooden and natural-fibre toys, to be marketed through schools. He was a craftsman in wood himself, aged about 55. He was employed in South London as a skilled cabinet-maker and for the last 20 years or more he had made, purely as a hobby, exquisite and universally admired toys sold at school Christmas Fairs. His wife was equally skilled in sewing and doll-making; it was planned that their new enterprise should be a husband-wife partnership.

The Financial Requirement.

Henry Smith asked for a loan of £8,000 in order to buy a small property and convert it into a workshop-with-flat-above. He had some £4,000 of his own and hoped to raise elsewhere a ten-year mortgage of £12,000; the property would cost £21,000 with about £3,000 conversion, much of the converting to be done by Smith himself. Toy manufacture and sales should begin, he thought, within six months of purchase, but the deal had to be closed *immediately* or the opportunity to buy the property would be lost.

Mercury's response.

We told Smith in the first place that there is no such thing as an immediate loan. Every transaction requires investigation and decisions – by lenders and by himself, the borrower. We began to formulate some questions in order to ascertain motivation, financial support and soundness, and social structure.

The intention was to provide children with imaginatively designed toys. The things he had made were esteemed by Waldorf teachers and would surely find a market – or rather take over a part of the existing market, which was already served by two makers of similarly styled toys.* Smith's good intentions might only be achieved at a cost to others. Was the financial package sound at all points? Mercury's investigations with orthodox mortgagees revealed that Smith would have trouble getting a 50% mortgage over 10 years, largely because of his age and because of the mixed residential and commercial use of the building. He probably needed more like £20,000 from Mercury; but he had made no provision for his own and his wife's support during the (non-productive)

---

* Waldorf teachers, i.e. teachers working in Rudolf Steiner schools, sometimes called Waldorf Schools, after the first Waldorf School founded by Steiner in Stuttgart.

conversion period of six months. Just to repay £20,000 @ 10% p.a. interest, with capital repayments spread evenly over the 10 years would require £4,000 in the first year, reducing to £2,200 in the final year. To maintain this, and to meet overheads and salary requirements would require an immediate turnover of £15,000 to £18,000 p.a. This would mean a six-day working week for the Smiths, with no holiday for the first five years, and would demand a very fast rate of work for a skilled craftsman accustomed to putting time into quality at the expense of quantity. In human terms, a high price to pay. To stretch the loan beyond 10 years – already very long – would take it beyond Smith's 65th year, which we were not prepared to do in any circumstances.

The character and talents of the people were all-important in coming to a decision. Both Smiths were steady, utterly reliable individuals whose honesty was vouched for from several quarters. But neither had any experience of managing a business: they could not read or maintain accounts, had given no thought to the legal form of the enterprise, had consulted no lawyer about the transfer of the property, and followed with some difficulty the financial reasoning of the Mercury agents who discussed the matter with them. They just had not considered what was really involved in borrowing and repaying. Their over-riding desire was to make a positive and healing contribution to life; alongside their courage in undertaking this was a strong sense of independence. (They had never owned their own property before, a fact of which they were almost ashamed.) Henry Smith's gifts did not include salesmanship, and he knew this; hence he insisted that his sales outlets would have to be Waldorf Schools and curative homes with, he believed, a built-in market. He did not see any need for active salesmanship among parents and felt that providing an outlet in a school would not create any significant additional work for anyone. He did not wish to use other outlets and had given no thought to the day when trade might grow to the point where he would need employees or partners.

He had not concerned himself with things like the legal structure of his enterprise and he conceived of the money as being 'in the bank' or 'the bank's to lend'; fair enough, in view of the prevailing image of financial institutions, but the Smiths found it hard to think of the legal or financial arrangements as being 'socially renewing' or otherwise; to them the only really renewing part of the enterprise was the *design of the toys*. In fact, legal and financial questions rather repelled both the Smiths; they simply wanted to make things with their hands.

The Decision:

Mercury turned down the Smith's request on several grounds:

a) economic conditions had thinned the market down so much that it was doubtful whether they could get enough income;

b) their lack of business know-how meant they would need a good deal of costly paid advice, or would need to take some costly crew on board – but clearly the economics of the business would not allow either course;

c) servicing and repaying the loan, while not crippling, would impose too great a strain;

d) most important, the entrepreneurs' vision of their task was too narrow to inspire others, too craft-centred and socially unaware to enable them to approach people and ask them to make deposits or supply guarantees as security: they simply saw no real human connection between themselves and the rest of the economy, and nothing the Mercury agents said could make any difference in this respect.

Further Consequences:

The two Mercury agents dealing with this case ventured the view that Henry Smith's (and to a lesser degree Mrs Smith's) real need was for a change in working environment and for a closer connection between his inner commitments and his work. The problem could only be solved by finding him a new job, preferably with like-minded people. If they had borrowed money and begun the new enterprise, the Smiths would probably have faced problems that would have made them regret their original impulse. The Mercury agents made some suggestions about alternative employment and despite some initial ill feeling, the Smiths followed up the leads and a year or so later Henry seemed happily engaged in new work for an established toymaker, and his wife was undertaking training as a needlework teacher; her training partly funded by gift money from a wealthy individual whom one of the Mercury agents had contacted – on his own initiative – after the refusal of the loan.

Case History Two: The Cathedral Waldorf School

The Idea and the People

In a medium-sized city in central England, a group of four families, all with children of pre-school age, wanted Waldorf education for their children. One of the mothers, Ellen Peters, had been trained as a Waldorf teacher and had a little experience in kindergarten and primary school teaching. The others had heard of Waldorf Education from lectures, reading or personal conversation, but had no direct experience of it. They were supported by an older woman who had sent her own child and grandchildren to a Waldorf school, and they established a weekly group meeting to study Waldorf education. It grew to a membership of sixteen and gradually became an initiative group, scraping together enough money to send a young local woman on a one-year training programme in Waldorf Nursery Class education. A modest programme of public lectures – about one a month – attracted as many as eighty people in one evening. They got a two-page spread in the local paper and set about raising funds by jumble sales, bring-and-buys and sponsored runs, but they barely paid for their own activities and the training of their nursery class teacher. They were going to need thousands to buy or build a school, and it was at this point that they approached Mercury. Could they borrow if the need arose? Naturally a hypothetical question can receive only a hypothetical answer. Basically it would depend on the strength of their local support, said Mercury.

The Financial Requirements.

A disused school building came on the market for £80,000 about a year after the initiative group had first contacted Mercury. The agents went to see it and discussed its suitability. There were pros and contras, of course, but the main concern from Mercury was security. If the building itself were taken as collateral, Mercury would be in the position of foreclosing should the repayments not be made. This was tantamount to holding the school to ransom, for the repayments depended on growth, and if growth were faltering or slow, a crisis could arise. The idea of a Borrowing Community (sometimes called a Loan Alliance) was discussed: if a group of, say, 40 families or individuals could be mustered, each prepared to donate £2,000 plus interest over a period of 5 years (under £10 per week) and to cross-guarantee one another, the loan could be made to the group. The point was made that it would have to be done swiftly, for the building would not stay on the market for long.

Mercury's Investigations:

Our two representatives arranged to meet the *whole* group of parents, and questions revealed the following picture. There were about 25 families in the school, with about 30 children, all aged 4 to 6 , in the kindergarten. They had developed a noticeable devotion to the school, and in the course of the evening, whenever the children were mentioned, there was a tone and look of mutuality, of common ground, a sense of reassurance that really they were all one family as far as the good of the children was concerned. When it came to money, however, their separation became evident; it could be seen that people hung back from making a commitment, and later it emerged that there were a significant number of families whose incomes would be severely stretched by school costs and a smaller number who sensed that they might be asked to give more than their fair share. The group heard about the Borrowing Community and, as frequently happens, were not sure they had grasped the notion. The agents repeated it step by step:

1) Each family borrows from Mercury a given sum (say £2,000).

2) This borrowed sum is donated to the school (under Deed of Covenant, using legitimate tax advantages).

3) Each family debt is repaid with interest to Mercury over five years.

4) Mercury's security is a set of cross-guarantees; that is, if there are forty members of the Borrowing Community, each borrowing £2,000, each borrower guarantees to provide 1/40 of every other borrower's debt in the event of default. This means that each borrower *guarantees* £2,000 in addition to *borrowing* £2,000, while his loan is guaranteed by all his fellow borrowers.

5) The whole is handled as one account and one transaction by Mercury, who deals with an individual or small group (as Treasurer) of the Borrowing Community. The Treasurer is responsible for seeing that repayments are made

regularly and that communication is alive and
well throughout.

There was considerable admiration expressed for the
dexterity of this technique, but it was clear that few if any
parents were prepared to commit themselves to the Community. The £80,000 building would not be achievable, and the
initiative group reconsidered the position. They would not be
able to establish any classes beyond kindergarten, and there
was no way of knowing when such an opportunity would arise
again. The initiative group seemed dispirited by the lack of
response, but the Mercury agents told them that this was not
unusual; in fact, the parents were held together only by their
children, not by a common ideal of education or common
sense of values. The initiative group would have to see if that
much stronger bond was there.

For the next year the search for new premises was therefore
not pursued. The emphasis was on the search for common
ground among parents; there were more talks and discussion
groups, but this time it was the members of the initiative
group and the kindergarten teacher and helpers who did the
intellectual work, not the visiting lecturers or Mercury agents.
They discussed new forms of school management such as
practised in Waldorf Schools (the College of Teachers) and
such things as child-parent and child-teacher relationships;
the attempt was made to create a strong sense of interdependence in spheres other than money. It was pointed out, for
example, that one TV-watching child may affect his class-
mates, that group norms are necessary for children even if
they can be oppressive for adult independence. No one quite
forgot the question of financing a new building, but it was
revived as a subject of discussion only when, after almost a
year, several parents outside the initiative group wanted to
talk about the future of their children, who would soon
outgrow the kindergarten. The fact that none could benefit
unless all participated became clear once again, but this time
there was less holding back. The question of the Borrowing

Community was re-evaluated, re-doubted, re-affirmed, and the initiative group was asked to approach Mercury once again to discuss it.

When the Mercury agents met with the whole parent group a second time, the central question was not 'How are we going to pay for our building?' but 'How can we best mobilise our resources in preparation for funding our school?'. The ensuing discussion showed the results of the year's work in communication and consciousness-raising; the Mercury representatives did more listening than talking. There were questions, puzzlement, struggles and contradictions, but the meeting showed an emerging community will, and in the end it was decided to establish a deposit account in Mercury in order to collect funds against the day when the school or the parents would have to borrow. A prospective Borrowing Community Treasury Group of three was appointed. The initiative group was asked to search for a building once again.

Four months later a new opportunity arose in the form of a nearby Church School's closure. It was put on the market and the initiative group examined it. It was much cheaper – about £30,000 – but would serve a growing school for only about four years, assuming a growth rate of one class per year. The parent body was apprised of the situation and with little delay expressed the will to go ahead. At the same time as finding the money, they would have to find a teacher. The decision to move forward was on this occasion something that came from the wish of a majority of those concerned, not the determination – clear-headed though it might be – of a few. This wish was underpinned by two convictions: first, that Waldorf education would be important enough in the world and in their children's lives to make sacrifices for; and second, that the establishment of the school would have to be a group effort and would work only if each individual were prepared to sink his personal interests in the group interest. These two ideas had developed in the course of discussions during the previous year, but they had arrived only at a cost: several parents had not shared these convictions and had placed their children in other schools. Other parents who came into the group during the year had not shared in the development of these ideas and did not find it easy to appreciate their importance. Rather they were aware of a slight cliquishness, even a sectarian mentality in the group. Clearly, finding a social balance that would permit freedom of thought alongside economic commitment was to be no easy task.

In the end, the cost of the building turned out to be more than £30,000, for inevitably there were a few repairs, the fees relating to the sale, and incidental expenses. The final figure was £34,000, which would include the first year's rates. Two of the new school's supporters were prepared to lend, unsecured and interest-free, £7,000 between them, but only for one year. Eighteen families formed the Borrowing Community. Each family's commitment would thus be £1,500 plus about 10% p.a. interest. The loan was made for four years, so this meant that the family budget would include £9.00 per week beyond their share of the running costs of the school. Some families found this a serious burden and several of them clubbed together to undertake commercial fund-raising to meet their obligations: jewellery-making, second-hand book sales, pottery and doll-making. They did not relieve only their own individual debts within the Borrowing Community but *one-another's*. 'Well,' said one, 'we're guaranteeing one another's debts in any case, and that's where the security for the loan lies. Working for one another is not all that difficult.' At the same time several families who could afford to donate more contributed to the pooled repayments to ease the burden for those who found it a struggle.

Mercury and the Cathedral Waldorf School had one more task: to find the deposits that would provide the loan. We were confident that once a Borrowing Community had been set up, it would not be difficult to find people prepared to lend. And we were right: when we advertised the project it was soon 80% subscribed, and we already had deposits earmarked for Waldorf Education in general, so a package could be made up with no difficulty. The important factor was that we could describe the solidarity of the parents as being the outstanding feature of the school, its strength and the basis for its future.

Further Consequences:

The Cathedral Waldorf School did not have an easy life of it in the following two years. They had great difficulty in finding and keeping teachers, and several of the founding families had to move away from the district. Such stresses had little effect on the functioning of the Borrowing Community, however; in two cases the loans of departing members were taken over by newcomers and in the third case the departing member maintained his repayments even though he was not going to benefit from the transaction.

The story is not yet finished, for the building purchased for the school had limitations, and when the school needs to move on or build an addition, it is clear that more money will have to be found. The Borrowing Community will have to grow and the support will have to be even stronger than before.

The two case histories just recounted are intended to demonstrate the necessity of community involvement in financing initiatives. The Mercury Provident Society is no different from any bank in this respect. What is a bank, after all? It is, as far as loan money is concerned, a collecting point; depositors leave their loan money in the hands of the banker so that he may decide where it should be invested. The banker is a representative of the communal financial will. The salient fact about Mercury's operation is that we try to make this as transparent and conscious as we can. Thus the source point of money for lending is as far as possible the will of the depositor, not the decision of the banker; the source of the security is the will of guarantors, not the value of capital assets involved in the transaction.

The social value of an enterprise, not the material value of its equipment, is the expression of its real worth. The passage of money from lender to borrower via the bank is an expression of confidence and to some degree an agreement about spiritual and cultural values. In its negative form – i.e. the desire *not* to finance certain industries or certain national policies – this is not new. Increasingly people are aware that any initiative, positive or negative, needs financial blood if it is to become flesh.

In the case of Henry Smith such wider social consciousness was lacking. His problem would not be solved by a loan, and it is just as well that his motives and initiative were tested by the bankers whom he asked for finance. The refusal was possibly an important step in his self-knowledge, but on this very account the bankers bear some responsibility in the development of his destiny. In the case of the Cathedral Waldorf School, the people at the heart of the initiative knew that without a social context expressed as material support, their efforts would go for nought. If the deposits, direct loans and guarantees were not forthcoming, then the social support would have proved itself to be no more than wishful thinking; there must be tests if an initiative wishes to show its strength. The bankers' role was catalytic; Mercury initiated the process of forming the Borrowing Community and provided the framework and financial harness for the initiative, and this may have done much to determine the parent-school relationships for years to come: school and environment were interacting with one another via the medium of money flowing through the channel provided by the bank. The Borrowing Community enabled supporters to *donate* money to the infant initiative. Like parents or guardians, they undertook to clothe the school, as it were, with no benefit to themselves. This is the healthiest possible relationship between a school and its supporters.

With a commercial initiative the relationship would be different. If Mercury were to lend, it would do so with the expectation that the initiative would be profitable, and if depositors shared this expectation, the loan would be made, interest rates being calculated as a balance between what the enterprise can afford and what the depositor needs as return. Security would best be provided in the form of guarantees, and the best possible guarantors would be potential (or actual) customers.

Profitability raises the important question of legal structure and ownership of an undertaking. The most common forms today seem to be designed to reward successful investors (the limited company) or successful entrepreneurs (sole ownership or partnership). Co-operatively owned producer enterprises are rare, and those where profitability is completely separated from ownership are even rarer. Mercury encourages this latter structure as much as possible: one solution has been to form a limited company and issue its shares to a charity or multi-purpose charitable trust, whose function is two-fold: first, to hold the shares as a neutral guardian of the entrepreneur against hostile ownership; and second, to receive and distribute (or use) profits in spiritual-cultural undertakings in need of gift money.

Throughout, the aim of Mercury in its financial dealings is to let investors' true intentions manifest themselves and to enable borrowers to see where their support comes from. The conventional bank manager's role hides depositor and borrower from one another. It is Mercury's intention to act as a sense-organ so that each may perceive the other more clearly. A working community will find its financial support only if it has the organs that enable it to look and to see what is normally not visible.

4. Money in Initiatives – Revenue Finance Between Purchase and Gift

Money circulates constantly through society, making visible an ever-moving 'sea of values', and making possible an extraordinarily complex interdependence among human beings all over the world. Every new organisation must find its place in this flow-pattern, and by doing so it will alter and contribute to the streams in which it stands. Managing the income and expenditure of an initiative means continually becoming conscious of the quality and quantity of money entering and leaving the organisation, and making adjustments to achieve the appropriate balance in the specific situation. In this 'conscious space' which an organisation can create amid the flow of money through society, choices may be made and priorities established: between income and expenditure lies the possibility of human freedom asserting itself.

The threefold aspect of money described earlier finds its reflection also in the ongoing finances of a project. The qualities of *purchase money* and *gift money* have been characterised. In between lies a realm in which the transfer of funds is regulated by *contractual arrangements*, written or unwritten. Loans are a simple example of this; the 'social contract' underlying taxation has also been mentioned. Contractual agreements assign rights and responsibilities to both parties; unlike gift or purchase, contract implies an ongoing relationship. *Purchase* is the exchange of what has been produced in the *past: gifts* make things possible for the *future: contracts* regulate the *present* state of relationship. This range of qualities of money will be perceptible in both the income and expenditure of most organisations. Identifying the particular configuration of sources of income and expenditure in one's own initiative, in terms of these three basic qualities, can become a fruitful starting point for penetrating the finances of an organisation with consciousness, and taking them in hand as an integral part of the initiative process.

The following chart shows some examples of gift money, 'contract money', and purchase money as these might appear as items in the revenue accounts of most organisations. Each institution will show its own specific configuration in this respect.

Revenue Finance Between Purchase and Gift

	Income	Expenditure	
Given by Sponsors	−Donations −Voluntary Subscriptions −Grants, subsidies, etc.	−Surpluses donated (→ future of society) −Taxation (compulsory gift) −Re-investment, training + development (→ future of organisation) −Distribution of profits	**Given to Beneficiaries**
	('Gift'→Future)		
Arranged with Clients	Fees: −negotiated −means tested −uniform scale of charges	−Staff community −Salaries −Hired labour −Pensions, etc.	**Arranged between Work-Partners**
	('Contract'⟷ Present)		
Paid by Customers	−Fixed prices for 'packaged' services −Sales of products	Costs: eg −Financial + professional services −Transport, fuel, power −Depreciation + Maintenance −Materials	**Paid to Suppliers**
	('Purchase'← Past)		

On the income side, we see money coming into the organisation from one or a combination of three main sources – *sponsors*, *clients*, and *customers*. *Sponsors* are those institutions and individuals prepared to support the initiative financially without asking anything in return (gift). *Clients* will make payments to the organisation in return for certain benefits, on an agreed *contractual* basis. *Customers* will pay a fixed *purchase price* for the goods or services produced.

On the expenditure side, we can see a reflection of these three kinds of relationships in the destination of the funds which flow out of an organisation. Starting from the 'purchase' aspect, we see first the true *costs* of an organisation; much work must be done by others outside the organisation before its own activity can take place. Those who do this work are the *suppliers* of the organisation, and they must be paid. A further portion of expenditure must be used to meet the needs of those who work *within* the organisation. There are many different bases for these arrangements, but whatever system is agreed upon, will for the present constitute a formal or informal *contract* among the *work-partners* in the initiative. A third category of expenditure arises when not all available funds are absorbed by the first two categories. The creation of surpluses or profits may be a major aim of the organisation, or may arise only incidentally; if it does not occur in any form, this may lead to severe restrictions on the development of the organisation and the people within it. Surpluses may be given away internally or externally; internal 'gifts' would include new investment within the organisation, as well as the provision of training and self-development facilities for staff, and the distribution of profits among employees and/or share-holders. In the case of non-charitable organisations, the State will take a portion of any financial surplus in taxation; this may be seen as a kind of 'compulsory gift' needed to fund those facilities which the State then provides 'free' for its citizens. Surpluses can, of course, also be freely and creatively gifted, through a trust or similar body, to meet human needs in any chosen social or cultural field. The 'gift' is thus a contribution towards the future of one's own organisation and/or of the wider society: those who receive this gift money, directly or indirectly, are the *beneficiaries* of the initiative.

Exercise: Budgeting

Financial planning in an initiative means lifting oneself out of the flow of day-to-day transactions, into the abstraction of figures, in order to become more consciously able to perceive and guide the economic consequences of one's activities. Often this process gives rise to explicit or implicit policy decisions, and these may or may not correspond to the overall direction agreed upon in other discussions. Sometimes people start to wonder: Are we in control of our project and its finances, or are the finances controlling us?

In such situations the following exercise can be helpful. First, try to set out the project's finances for a recent period, with figures, in the 'three-fold' form shown in the chart on page 119. Place items in the different areas according to how you actually regard them: for instance, do you see the services of part-time or junior employees as a cost, like the electricity bill, or are these people part of a 'social contract' arrangement which includes human considerations? There will of course be grey areas, but this 'placing' of items (income as well as expenditure) can already reveal much about the attitudes underlying financial policy.

This can be made more explicit by working with the following questions:

Continued

Income:

1. What are our products? Are they still attractive in quality and price? Are we still in touch with our market's requirements? What are realistic targets for sales income?

2. Who are our clients? Are the agreements we have with them still mutually satisfactory, or do some things need re-negotiating? In what ways do we aim to deepen or broaden these relationships, and what effect will this have on our income?

3. Who are our sponsors? What aspects of our activity are people most willing to support with gifts? How can we develop this support, and what financial expression of it can be expected?

Expenditure:

1. Which of our costs are *fixed*, i.e. related to *time,* and which are *variable,* i.e. related to our actual *activity*? What 'standard of living' – physical environment, facilities etc. – does our initiative need? Does our spending pattern reflect our true priorities in this realm?

2. On what basis do we support our staff, ourselves, each other? Do these arrangements correspond to the relation we want to have between ourselves? What are our guiding values in distributing resources to individuals?

Continued

3. Who are the beneficiaries of our enterprise? What are our developmental aims – for them, for ourselves, for the project? What investment in physical and/or human *resources* will be required?

Handling Purchase Money

This is the most apparently 'objective' use of money – in straight-forward buying and selling, people can feel on firm ground. Budgeting can and should be accurate here, both of income and expenditure. Those responsible will ask themselves questions such as:

- If a higher quality product is more expensive, what level of quality and cost is truly appropriate to the needs of our customers?
- What level is appropriate in supplying our own organisation?
- Production and consumption use up resources, some scarce: what is our responsibility to the Earth and our fellow humans in what we use and what we waste?
- Do we wish to charge the maximum price for our products (market forces) or can we, perhaps in dialogue with clients, work towards a concept of 'true price', i.e. what we need to receive in order to continue producing on a satisfactory basis?

The purchase principle, perhaps because most accessible and transparent, often tends to spill over into realms where it is not appropriate, and produce distortions; thus we speak, for instance, of a 'labour market', and even a 'money market' as if labour and capital were commodities to be bought and sold, like carrots. Purchase money tries to present all transactions as purchases, often thereby obscuring their true nature. For example, a pension fund is a set of contractual agreements whereby those at work now support those who have retired. Provided the fund continues, they can expect to be supported themselves later. In reality there are rights and responsibilities involved here, but no commodities; yet we often think of 'buying into' such a scheme, in purchase terms – and advertising may present it as a 'good bargain'. In managing the finances of an initiative, then, it will be important to distinguish the true *costs* of the operation (i.e. the cost of commodities purchased from outside), from contractual arrangements, made internally or externally. This distinction, by re-asserting the freedom of people to negotiate the financial relationships they want, can defuse much of the power and powerlessness often experienced in relation to money.

Handling Contractual Money

Contractual money is created and moved as a result of *agreements* worked out between people. These sometimes take the form of an apparent exchange (e.g. so much money for so much work) and sometimes tend more to the 'gift' element (e.g. a deed of covenant). Typically, contractual money expresses a *state of relationship* between the parties involved. *The intention to create and maintain a certain type of relationship* is the guiding principle here.

For instance, an institution providing educational or therapeutic facilities to its clients may wish simply to sell those services on a semi-commercial basis (e.g. a private language or secretarial school), in which case the appropriate form will be a fixed 'price' for a certain course of lessons or treatment. However, an increased sense of responsibility to clients may lead to the granting of scholarships or reductions for those less able to pay, such as the elderly or unemployed. This 'sliding scale' of fees may be means-tested or even individually negotiated. Here, a quite different principle from that of sale and purchase becomes visible. When, from the other side, the responsibility of clients and supporters increases in the same way, one may see 'contracts' such as voluntary subscriptions or regular contributions entered into, which are more akin to gifts.

Many voluntary and political organisations work in this way; a charitable trust may have a nominal subscription fee conferring certain rights and privileges on its members, whilst also relying heavily on donations. A campaigning organisation may give some guidelines to its supporters, which take account of personal circumstances – waged/unwaged/family, etc. An independent school which wishes to move away from the 'selling' of education may ask for a percentage of family income from those who send their children to the school ... and so on.

A similar spectrum of alternative arrangements can be seen *within* an organisation, in the way in which financial support is provided for its staff. It is usual in our society to base remuneration for work on a person's capacities, e.g. skills, seniority, level of responsibility, etc., but some newer social initiatives are trying to move away from this 'purchase of capacities' towards an increased mutual responsibility in providing for each other's needs. Such projects will tend to assume a high level of non-financial motivation among staff, which 'releases' funds from the incentive function, so that money can be used more effectively to meet human needs. It is in principle quite uneconomic to have to 'bribe' people into working hard!

CLIENTS/SPONSORS

- -

Fixed fees   Fixed subscriptions/   Means test   Arranged   Donations
premiums   Contributions

'Purchase'   Contractual Arrangements   'Gift'

INSTITUTION

Individuality   Mutuality

Fixed salaries   Needs test   Arranged   Incomes   Direct Provision
based on ability/   needs-based   community
status   salaries

- -

STAFF/DEPENDANTS

In commercial organisations, the concept of 'added value' can be a helpful starting point from which to move away from the image of labour as a *cost*. In simple terms, added value can be defined as the difference between the total income of a firm from sales, and the cost of goods and services supplied from outside. This difference is the value added by the work of those in the organisation, using its capital facilities.

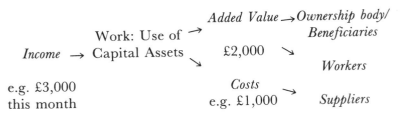

		Added Value →	*Ownership body/*
			Beneficiaries
Income →	Work: Use of ↗		
	Capital Assets ↘	£2,000 ↘	
			Workers
e.g. £3,000		*Costs* ↗	
this month		e.g. £1,000	*Suppliers*

The added value thus generated can then be divided on any agreed contractual basis between the staff of the firm, with a portion allocated to the trustees or owners of the capital assets for development and other 'gift' purposes. This 'contractual sharing of added value', which has been adopted for example by a printing co-operative that I know of, effectively overcomes the indignity and alienation experienced, often unconsciously, by those whose work is treated as a commodity. In non-commercial projects, the amounts available to support staff will relate to the *recognition* which their activity receives from wider society, rather than the creation of added value, but internally there will be similar decisions to be made regarding the criteria for distribution.

These criteria may combine elements of 'need', seniority, level of skill, and responsibility, etc. in any chosen form. A small woodworking firm, for instance, whose salary structure has grown rather haphazardly, has recently started experimenting with the use of three main criteria – skill, responsibility, and need. Within each of these, different levels have been identified which can be immediately recognised and related to – in this way the workers can find their own place and basis for remuneration in the firm. Something like the following table then emerges:

Criterion	*Levels*		
SKILL	'Apprentice'	'Journeyman'	'Master'
RESPONSIBILITY	For own work only	For a department or aspect	For the totality of the firm
NEED	Single person	'Post-family'	Family to support

'Needs-based' arrangements may take the form, e.g. of 'needs-tested' or individually agreed salaries, of incomes communities whose members draw from a common pool of money, or of residential communities where most needs are directly provided for the co-workers of the institution. One danger with 'needs-based' systems can be that 'needs' quickly become interpreted as 'subsistence level', and the idealism of the co-workers is exploited (often by themselves!) to conceal the fact that the project is basically under-financed. Unless people are substantially freed from moral pressure in determining their own needs, such arrangements can be experienced as a straitjacket rather than a liberation. The aim here must be to find the appropriate outer arrangements to express and sustain the actual relationship which the staff want (and are *able*) to have to each other and to their organisation. The 'purchase' end of this spectrum emphasises *self-responsibility*; the separation of remuneration from individual performance emphasises *mutual responsibility*. Each project must find its own way of balancing these two principles.

Accurate budgeting for contractual finance is perfectly possible, at least in the short and medium-term, as soon as the chosen arrangements are agreed and clear. They must also be specific. For instance, to state that: 'Staff can draw money to meet their private needs from our current account', may be fine as a statement of principle, but its operation will quickly become chaotic unless it is translated into a definite arrangement such as: 'Any two of three mandated members may sign cheques on the current account to meet staff needs, up to a maximum of £35,000 p.a.. Not more than £4,000 may be drawn in any single month. The resulting financial picture will be reviewed quarterly in the staff meeting.'

A group of teachers I worked with decided to set up a community bank account, into which a lump sum would be paid each term by the school where they worked. They would each have a 'cash card' with which to draw from this account, and meet regularly to share their assessments of their own needs, make informal agreements as to the amount each would draw in a given period, and formulate their joint request to the school for the following term. In this way, the individual aspect of staff finance was placed entirely in the hands of those directly affected – only the total amount required became the concern of the school Council responsible for approving the overall budget. In general, this arrangement works well – it is experienced not as *easier*, but as more 'real' than a conventional salary system.

On such a basis, contractual finance can be handled both humanely and accurately. Similar comments would apply to, for example, the terms of a private loan, or undertakings from a support or client group to provide income for the project. Reliability in budgeting rests not on the market, as with purchase money, but on mutual trust and responsibility between specific people – staff, clients and supporters.

Fundamental Social Law

In a community of human beings working together the well-being of the community will be the greater, the less the individual claims the proceeds of the work he has done himself; i.e. the more of these proceeds he makes over to his fellow-workers and the more his own requirements are satisfied not out of his own work done, but out of work done by others.

- Every institution in a community of human beings that is contrary to this law will inevitably engender in some part of it, after a while, suffering and want.
- It is a fundamental law which holds good for all social life with the same absoluteness and ne-

Continued

cessity as any law of nature within a particular
field of natural causation.

- It must not be supposed, however, that it is
  sufficient to acknowledge this law as one for
  general moral conduct, or to try and interpret it
  into the sentiment that everyone should work for
  the good of his fellow-men.
- This law only finds its living, fitting expression in
  actual reality, when a community of human
  beings succeeds in creating institutions of such a
  kind that no one can ever claim the results of his
  own labour for himself, but that they all, to the
  last fraction, go wholly to the benefit of the
  community.

  And he, again, must himself be supported in
  return by the labour of his fellow-men. The
  important point is, therefore, that working for
  one's fellow-men, and the object of obtaining so
  much income, must be kept apart, as two
  separate things.

Extracts from: *Anthroposophy and the Social Question*
Rudolf Steiner 1905/1906

Handling Gift Money

We generally think of 'gifts' in terms of small-scale altruism –
coins in a charity collecting box, or Christmas presents for
family and friends. But in fact all money which is used to meet
social or cultural requirements, without demanding anything
– economically – in return, is moving according to the 'gift'
principle. Funding for education, medicine, the arts, religion,

welfare benefits – this money is all 'given': the values it represents are not immediately needed to support economic producers. In many cases the responsibility for the gifting process is taken over by the State, which uses income from taxation (compulsory gifts) to support, and also control, certain cultural and social activities. This can become an anonymous, bureaucratic and even oppressive system.

Many small-scale initiatives, however, will have the opportunity and the need to handle gift money which is made available by relatively free human decisions, especially in cases where state sponsorship is not available. Gifts will need to be attracted perhaps both for the establishment of capital assets and for some proportion of ongoing revenue. A key aspect here will be *communication*. Gift funding can flow freely when needs are made visible in the right way, in the right place, and when an appropriate social framework is seen to be available to receive and use it. An appeal for gifts must touch the *inner* needs and impulses of the sponsor, not his outer requirements as in the case of a purchase. It must therefore express in imaginative form, the inner aims and values of the project seeking support, and communicate these 'heart to heart'.

Self-examination is therefore the first step towards finding gift money. Do we have the energy and commitment to communicate our vision so that others can become enthused by it? Are our aims clear and important enough – not only to ourselves! – to attract the support needed? Can we kindle a real social warmth around the project? Are our proposed activities really wanted by others?

Secondly, in seeking gift finance, it can often be helpful to 'think backwards' by imagining oneself in a situation where the required funds *had* been made available: where would they have come from? Every individual and organisation not engaged in economic production, is in fact supported by an invisible network of conscious and/or unconscious sponsors: in actively seeking gift funding, one needs to make this actual and potential web of connections visible to oneself. Try to form as vivid and full a picture as possible of one's past, present and possible future connections in this respect. Can one imagine certain specific sources of gifts, providing the required amount over the required period? For example, a student seeking sponsors for a year's course might imagine a small grant from one of three foundations known to have supported previous students on the same course, plus a few pounds a week from, say, six out of ten friends or relatives who could be approached. If a number of different combinations can be imagined to find the funds needed, this will give increased chances. In many cases the personal connections of those involved will be as decisive as the worthiness of their aims.

The third step will be to assess these imaginative pictures. Are they realistic? If not, certain expectations may have to be adjusted. It is vital to eliminate wishful thinking at this stage, to move from: 'If only someone would give us £x...' to: 'If these people give what we can reasonably ask of them...'. If this is achieved, then the fourth step of approaching potential sponsors becomes a kind of active research into one's own and the project's destiny. If the aims and needs of the initiative are communicated without sentimentality or manipulation, then one can receive gifts without incurring moral obligations. This may be important when personal connections are involved.

The truly free gift is a rare thing in our society. In many cases the gifting process is mediated and determined by a political process: in many others, an apparent gift is in fact a concealed form of purchase, as in much commercial 'sponsorship' of sport, etc. Organisations which are in a position to generate or mediate the flow of gift money can in this realm directly create freedom for others. In order to fulfil this potential, they will need to act scrupulously both in the exercise of their own decision-making responsibilities, and in resisting the temptation to extend this responsibility beyond the moment when the gift is made, by attaching strings or conditions which would inhibit the free use of what has been set free in this way, by those people who carry the impulse or institution which has been judged worthy of support.

Social and cultural initiatives and their supporters have an important task for the future, in creating forms and procedures, whereby the flow of gift money to support what is seen to be needed, becomes an *objective process* alongside the spontaneous expression of generosity. When this happens, reliable budgeting will be possible in this realm also, and the 'faith' on which it is based will not be 'blind faith', but an objective faith in the spiritual impulses underlying human decisions.

5. *Sense-Organs for Money*

Money has a peculiarly direct connection to the human Ego. It affects us in ways that can be intimidating, paralysing, fascinating, fructifying. It tests our courage and integrity. It must serve our initiatives, but often appears or attempts to control them. It facilitates our organisational and individual lives, but may, if we allow it, take on a life of its own. Its potential for social harm can be overcome only by conscious mutual support between human beings.

We have spoken of the bank as a 'sense-organ', and the need for initiatives to develop organs for 'what is not normally visible'. We have also tried to show that one can develop a sense for the different qualities which money can take on. In moving from purchase money through contractual money to gift money, the sense-organs required become progressively more inward. Our judgements regarding *purchase money* can be based on market research, on evaluation of products and on dialogue with customers and suppliers. A sense for the appropriate arrangements in *contractual finance* can only be gained through discussions with a background of mutual trust, interest and knowledge. In seeking *gift finance,* we need to conduct a vigorous research into our own motivation and destiny. In these ways the power of money can be harnessed towards the fulfilment of our social and spiritual aims.

Chapter Six

The Conscious Development of Initiatives

Christopher Schaefer

The Nature of Initiatives and Organisations

Underlying the following discussion of initiatives, and indeed other portions of this book, are three basic assumptions. The first is that all initiatives and organisations are human creations, no matter how old and well established. They are created by people with an idea conceived in response to a perceived need, and they are continuously being modified by other people's ideas and actions. A school, a café, a company, may well carry something of the personality of the founders, but it is changed by the ideas and aspirations of those who now share the responsibility. So we live and move in a world created by nature and in a large and increasingly complex institutional world created by people.

The second assumption is that this organisational world of banks, shops, restaurants, schools, and government agencies is one in which each initiative, like a human being, goes through characteristic phases of development. Organisations are not mechanical systems but, as Kenneth Boulding and others have noted, are *living systems* with phases of crisis, adaptation, growth and development.[1] This means that organic metaphors such as seed, stalk, bud and flower, or childhood, adulthood and old age, are more relevant to the life cycle of organisations than mechanical metaphors such as input, output, clockwork or a smooth running engine. It also implies the third assumption, namely that one of the central tasks of initiative takers is keeping the organisation alive and developing as a healthy living organism.

In working in schools, shops, and small companies I am frequently surprised how little awareness initiative takers have about their whole organisation and about its stage of development and how relieved they are when they recognise that their organisation, while unique, shares characteristic phases of crisis and development with other organisations. The following description is devoted to giving a general picture of the phases of an initiative's development over time, as an aid for individuals to more consciously shape and develop their organisations. The picture presented in no way seeks to deny the uniqueness of individual initiatives, but rather to describe the characteristic challenges and opportunities which exist in the life cycle of most organisations.

The Pioneer Phase – Improvising in Response to Needs

As has previously been noted, for an initiative to succeed over time there needs to be an individual or a group responding to a real need, a number of capable people willing to work hard, and some organisational and financial basis for the initiative. Looked at from the viewpoint of the life phases of an organisation, one can say there is a gestation period when one or more individuals are walking around with an idea – an idea which is slowly ripening. This gestation period may be shorter or longer – often it is deeply connected with one individual's life and destiny. Henry Ford knew he wanted to be an engineer at twelve. He also knew he wanted to found his own automobile company when he was in his late twenties. But it took him until forty to finally create the Ford Motor Company.[2]

Following the gestation period is a moment of birth – when the school first opens its doors, the company delivers its first product, or the toy store has its first customer. This is a very important moment in the biography of all initiatives and it should be celebrated like a birthday. Usually this is done, often unconsciously, through a party, a festive meal, or even just saving the first dollar or pound earned by the new business. However, if this can be done consciously, as a foundation or a birth ceremony, inviting friends, customers, and helpers, it will help to get the new baby off to a good start.

Frequently I have experienced that the situation at the birth moment of the initiative gives clues to the characteristic challenges or problems an organisation will confront in its life history. For example, a well-established school started many years ago with a group of experienced Waldorf teachers and a local headmistress who knew very little about the principles of Waldorf education. Its identity as a Waldorf school has since that time been periodically challenged by both teachers and parents. The Ford Motor Company resulted from a conflict between Henry Ford and his earlier partners. His and, I believe, the company's relationship to the industry as a whole, and to the Detroit community in particular, had a troubled atmosphere for many years, in part because of this early rift. Another school I was once associated with was conceived and founded entirely by a strong parent and community group without significant involvement by the first teachers. The result was that finding the right relationship between parents and teachers was a struggle in the school's history.

If the new initiative flourishes, it enters a period which is analogous to childhood; vibrant, exciting, full of surprises and of growth. Co-workers are involved in many activities, routine is limited and the direction of the initiative is clear. It is a time full of ups and downs – a mood similar to the early twenties in an individual's life.

A couple who started a Futon manufacturing and retail business only a few years ago gave a picture which describes many early initiatives which have gotten off to a successful start: endless activity in deciding on staff, setting wage levels, ordering supplies, supervising production, keeping the books, getting bank loans, planning future activities and occasionally stopping to catch a breath. They also mentioned two qualities essential to any starting enterprise: concern for the quality of their Futon (cotton) bedding, and doing their utmost to assure customer satisfaction. The same qualities apply to a new school, a café, or any endeavour. Its reputation rests on the satisfaction of its clients, customers or parents. If it provides a quality service or product, it will generally thrive.

Having a concern about quality and client satisfaction means that a new initiative, a pioneer organisation, has to act like a large sense organ, continuously monitoring the satisfaction of those it serves while at the same time sensing how the initiative is functioning internally. If shop hours are not regular, or if a school is unable to maintain discipline, interest and support will begin to decline.

Sometimes people have the question whether it is better to start an initiative alone or together with others. In reality this is never an abstract question; a couple will decide to open a furniture store, one individual to start a college, or two partners – one in production, one in sales – to begin a manufacturing company. In the past a single individual – a pioneer – tended to start a new venture and others then joined him or her, attracted by the personality and vision of the individual. Now, pioneer or initiative groups are more common. They need to be certain that they have a common vision and are equally committed with their time and energy. Absent and half-hearted initiative takers are not readily accepted by those who are in it full-time. Also the group should not be too large and should be capable of working together. If these conditions are met, then a group of individuals – because of their combined talents and wider set of human connections – has a greater potential than a single pioneer.

As the pioneer organisation grows, it has a number of characteristic qualities which one can observe in organisations as diverse as shops, schools, companies, and therapeutic centres:

- It is generally of small to medium size, although I have worked with a community college with a teaching staff of 500, still in its pioneer phase.
- It has a shallow flexible structure with a limited hierarchy. Key decision-makers are often involved in the full scope of organisational activities.
- It is person-oriented, rather than function-oriented. If you ask a pioneer about his or her organisation, you will usually be told that Tom does publicity, Mary, craft therapy, Steve, counselling, and so on.
- Leadership is personal and direct with people generally knowing who makes what decisions. However, throughout the initiative's growth there is the need to clarify the role of the central carrying group in relation to specific task groups and supporters. This is especially important and problematical in initiatives largely dependent on volunteer help.
- Decision-making is intuitive. Things are decided more by hunch or by feel than through a long process of rational analysis. This style of arriving at decisions usually means that the pioneer organisation is able to respond rapidly to changes in the environment. If you ask some of the early staff how they joined the initiative, they will tell you that they met with the key person or persons and more often than not talked about subjects quite unrelated to their field of specialisation.

One person I know was hired to establish a new psychology department in a college. He spent most of an hour talking about back yard grills and how best to build them, and was then offered the job.

- The pioneer organisation has a family atmosphere about it. Everyone contributes as they are able and most of the staff have a strong sense of loyalty to the founding group, and to the initiative.
- Motivation and commitment in a pioneer organisation are high.
- The goals of the organisation are implicit — carried in the minds and personalities of the carrying group.[3]

This phase of an organisation's life is exciting, somewhat insecure, and very creative. It is really about developing something out of an idea, a hope, and seeing it grow into an institution with services or products, a physical space, and staff. Another way of describing this is to say that one is bringing a child into the world — a child with its unique personality — full of vitality and potential. Very often one has the feeling of being helped; as if some entity wishes to have an abode on earth and is doing its best to make this possible. I believe that this is indeed the case and that developing an initiative is a process of providing the body, or sheaths, for a new identity to emerge. Consequently, the motives and aims of the initiative are important in determining what identity, what being is attracted to it. Seen from this perspective, the pioneer phase of an initiative is the time in which something of the identity, of the ego, of the initiative becomes visible, and the first home or physical body is created.

As the initiative grows, a number of problems begin to appear. This may be five, ten, or even twenty-five years after its beginning. One of the issues is size; not everyone knows everyone anymore. New people join the organisation in substantial numbers and do not share the joys and struggles of the early days, having no relation to the institutions's past or the people who made it what it is. Another issue is that new structures of decision-making are needed to cope with increased size and complexity. Leadership often becomes unclear and motivation decreases. A sense of uncertainty, of crisis exists.[4]

In many smaller initiatives in the cultural and service areas this crisis of the pioneer phase includes some of the following phenomena:

- A loss of confidence in leadership. Increasing criticism, usually by newer people, about the 'autocratic' and 'irrational manner' in which decisions are made. Newer people have little relationship to the starting situation and the sacrifices that the original group made in getting things going. In some cases, these issues are also generational with a new generation of people wanting to both have more influence and wanting to work in new ways.
- An unclarity about goals and directions which at an earlier time were embodied in the carrying group. Then there was a personal relationship, and if there was a question, everybody knew who to go to. I remember attending a faculty meeting in an educational institution and watching all heads turn toward one person when a question of significance arose. In the absence of close personal relationships, the need for clearly understood goals and policies arises. What was implicit and personal needs to become explicit and objective.
- The need for a definition of responsibilities and decision-making authority. When things are smaller and informal one decision-making centre is adequate; but if you have a kindergarten, a lower school and a high school, or upper school,

who has what responsibilities? In a college, what is the relationship between the teaching faculty and the administration, or between the departments or divisions? In a store, how will purchasing, accounting, merchandising and hiring be divided in an orderly fashion? Such questions become burdensome and indeed become the source of conflicts.

In larger service and economic institutions, similar issues appear although often they focus on:

- more rational approaches to marketing and sales;
- rationalising and centralising staff functions such as finance, personnel, information systems, and marketing at the expense of operational autonomy;
- dissatisfaction with intuitive personalistic approaches to people;
- the need for more expertise, and more professionalism in production to cope with new technology.

In both large and small institutions the crisis of the pioneer phase is perplexing and painful. The need for change is recognised but its direction and how to achieve it often remains obscure. It is in such circumstances that a developmental picture can help, not as a prescription but as a rough road map so that at least the nature of the next landscape is discernible.

Differentiation: The Challenge of Diversity with Consciousness

The challenge of the phase of differentiation is how one can move from the personal, intuitive, improvising mode of a smaller pioneer organisation to a more objective, clear and functional way of meeting a larger organisation's objectives. In my experience, there is a trade-off between consciousness and form in meeting this challenge. The more conscious people are of goals and policies – the direction and guiding principles of an organisation – the less there is the need for rigid forms and control mechanisms. However, in the absence of shared goals and policies, hierarchical principles, procedural handbooks, and rigid reporting relationships seem to become imperatives.

Cultural institutions such as schools, professional organisations, therapy centres and the like often resist the pressures for greater functional clarity, attempting to muddle through. This tendency is quite pronounced in faculty-run schools, partly because most teachers have limited administrative and organisational experience. The trend in most businesses is the other way – replacing people by systems and so rationalising operations that individuals feel like a cog in the proverbial machine. The tendency to muddle through, to cling to a vague hope of the old unity, generates chaos and the struggle for power between individuals. The opposite emphasis subordinates people to logic and robs individuals of their creativity.

The central question for all types of institutions in this phase of development is to bring about functional differentiation without sacrificing human creativity and commitment. Achieving this balance, and entering a healthy differentiation process, involves paying attention to the following organisational needs:

I: Renewing the Identity of the Initiative

Renewing the identity and purpose of the initiative by developing a vision of the future and clear mission statement. This means a renewed dialogue with the spirit, developing a vision – a struggle for the original and now newly willed central aims of the organisation. The process of developing a vision of the future is akin to an individual asking him or herself what is really central to their life. It should involve many people in different parts of the organisation so that a commonly shared sense of direction emerges.

A college I know took over a year to develop an image of the future including faculty, administrators and support staff in the process. While lengthy, it was time well spent as it generated a new hope and commitment. In many organisations suggesting such a process raises fears. Will teachers and administrators, or top managers and supervisors, not want totally different things? I have never experienced this to be the case. Generally, people see the same organisational reality and share a common picture of the values they want to pursue in the future. In this process of renewing the culture, the identity, of the institution, it is essential to also call to mind the initiative's biography, the rich texture of its history, personalities, failures and successes.

II: Leadership Functions

In conjunction with renewing the organisations's sense of purpose, there is a need to create a new understanding of the different functions of leadership. What are the differences between goals and policies and where and how does evaluation and review take place? Such differences are seldom understood and yet such a differentiation in awareness, in consciousness, needs to be present to provide a healthy basis for differentiation in form and function.

While there are different ways of describing the main leadership functions in organisations, they often include the following aspects:

1) Goal Setting
2) Policy Formulation
3) Establishing Plan and Procedures
4) Integrating Functions
5) Organising and Executing Work Activities
6) Innovating and Renewing

7) Evaluating and Reviewing

Goal setting consists of setting long and medium term goals for the initiative. It is a central responsibility of those guiding the organisation, although ideally those in less responsible positions should be involved.

Policies are different from goals. They provide a framework, a set of guidelines, according to which individuals can make decisions and act. Examples are policies on hiring or promotion, purchasing, sales, remuneration, and the like. This applies to schools and shops as well as to companies. If a hiring committee at a Waldorf school has an agreed upon policy that Waldorf-trained teachers with at least a half year's practicum are essential qualifications, then they have something to go on.

Establishing plans and procedures for particular work activities can be done if goals and policies are shared. The scholarship committee of a school can develop its plans and procedures knowing what policy there is on financial aid and what restrictions exist in terms of the projected budget (a statement of financial goals). A small manufacturing company can plan production if annual goals and a marketing plan exists. In short, the delegation of responsibility becomes possible to sub-units, committees, or even to individuals, within a broad goal and policy framework. Developing such a framework is, of course, helped when the organisation has already reviewed its sense of purpose.

The first three functions of leadership have been mentioned. They tend to be the responsibilities of all or most of the professional staff in smaller service or professional organisations. The fifth function, that of *organising and executing work activities*, belongs to the whole organisation, but the focus is on the worker rather than the supervisor. In a school it is the teachers or in a café the cook and the waitresses who need to organise and carry out the myriad of daily activities. Likewise, *innovation and renewal* are everyone's responsibility, although for the organisation as a whole it tends to lie with those individuals or groups having a central leadership role.

Evaluation and review is usually understood as financial review and quality control in product organisations and seldom is paid much attention to in other types of institutions. Yet it is absolutely central to an initiative's learning and development. In schools or service agencies, in shops, farms or medical facilities, it should be like an extended New Year reflection. How has this year gone? What successes and failures have we had? Why did things go wrong in this class or with this particular product? What can we improve upon next year? What new activities can we engage in? Questions of this type are vital, and the more members of an organisation that are engaged in them the more responsible the work community that is created.

The fourth function mentioned, that of *integration*, is like five, six and seven; everyone's concern, yet it tends to fall heavily on those having a supervisory function. They must relate more general goals and principles to specific tasks.

Bringing about an awareness of the leadership functions in an organisation is by itself not enough – they must be exercised. Where and by whom are long and medium term goals set? How are they communicated and responded to by other parts of the organisation? I have worked with some clients where goals were set but it was largely a paper exercise for outside consumption, and people within the initiative knew little about it.

Policy formulation is equally important. Where and by whom are policies to be defined? Plans and procedures are established and carried out in many parts of an organisation, as are the other functions, yet what is important is that people are aware of what functions of leadership are being exercised by whom and how the results are communicated to the rest of the institution.

If we step back from this functional description and ask what really lies behind the differentiation process in organisations, then we can say that the soul of the organisation is being developed. This inevitably involves multiplicity and differentiation just as in the individual the soul development of the twenties and thirties manifests through becoming aware of the complexity of thoughts, emotions and intentions. This process of differentiation is difficult for many initiatives because it involves some task specialisation. But if overall goals and policies are shared by people in the initiative, then the conscious division of tasks can take place so that the whole benefits.

III: Functional Specialisation

A third organisational need in the differentiation stage is that of functional specialisation and structural clarity. In self-administered schools there is a need to differentiate the upper or high school from the lower grades and from the pre-school. Administration, records, accounting, fundraising, and publicity activities need to be consciously picked up. Committees need to be established as everything can no longer be decided and implemented by one decision-making group. In my experience, the following types of functions need the attention of individuals or small groups in schools and other cultural initiatives:

1) Curriculum Review and Planning
2) Festivals and Special Events
3) Hiring
4) Teacher Evaluation
5) Enrolment
6) Fund-Raising
7) Finance and Budget
8) Buildings and Grounds
9) Publicity

This list is by no means exhaustive, as there are schools with twelve or more committees, not counting the Board, the faculty meeting or the college of teachers.

What is true for schools is also true for shops, curative

homes, therapy centres and the like. The phase of differentiation can also be called an administrative phase, in which what was done semi-consciously to make things run in the early years now needs conscious attention.

As was pointed out in Chapter Three, an important principle during this phase of development is that of giving clear mandates and responsibilities to sub-groups or committees of an initiative. This means that each committee needs to have clear terms of reference regarding the tenure and areas of responsibility. What often happens in self-administered initiatives is that committees are set up but that central decision-making groups have not established policies and are not really willing to delegate. Consequently issues which should be decided by the committee are continuously brought back to the central group and a process of second-guessing and criticism takes place. It requires discipline and clarity to establish and stick to mandates. This is the essence of 'Republican' leadership which E. Lehrs, among others, has argued for persuasively.[5]

The need for specialisation and functional clarity is even greater in product organisations. While in the pioneering stage marketing, sales, production, technical innovation, and finance may have been handled by a partnership of two or three people, this is no longer adequate. Marketing and finance, to name two examples, are important areas of specialisation in their own right and require professionals with support staff to be handled adequately. The same is true of personnel, information systems, shipping, purchasing, and a host of other areas. This means that in addition to operating line responsibilities, staff functions need to be developed to provide the expertise necessary for the organisation to function effectively. Here, too, clarity of policies and procedures allows differentiation without excessive control.

IV A Change in Leadership and Decision–Making Styles

A new technical system will effect social relationships and financial outcomes. A new product line requires investment, training, shifts in work patterns and new equipment. Consequently, any important decision needs to consider the consequences in these three areas and to include those measures or activities which will assure an integrated approach. Most importantly, the human impact of change needs to be considered and human needs taken more consciously into account in the integration phase.

If the mentioned organisational needs of renewed purpose, new leadership functions, clear structures, and new style have been met, then an organisation can enter a healthy differentiation process in which new functional structures are balanced by a new and different consciousness. The organisation will then manifest the following characteristics, while still making an appeal to human creativity and involvement:

1) Increased Size
2) Clear Policies and Procedures
3) Differentiated Structures, Mandates and Staff-Line Distinctions
4) A higher level of Professionalism
5) Functional rather than Personal Leadership
6) Rational, Analytical Decision-Making
7) Greater Clarity of Work Activities

Institutions may develop and refine differentiated forms and procedures for many years, sometimes employing the latest technology in doing so. This period is analogous to middle adulthood and carries a soul orientation appropriate to the period of 28-35 in an individual's biography. Planning and rational analysis are most pronounced in this period of life, and in the term a 'differentiated organisation'. As one would also expect, many people in their thirties feel more at home in this type of organisational environment than in the riskier pioneer institution.

As with the thirty year old, a differentiated organisation runs the risk of too much rationality. The need for social contact, for a fostering of human relationships is very important. Can the staff of a well established school continue with the vitality of spiritual work and create regular opportunities for meeting, for sharing meals, for knowing each other? Can a group of architects or workers in a shop create possibilities for the soul of the initiative to live? Soul differentiation needs to be balanced by conscious attention to 'ensoulment' to fun, as well as work.

Many organisations reach this phase in their life cycle, often unconsciously and with great struggle. Yet it is clear that this phase too has its limitations, its period of crisis, as anyone who has worked in a large corporation or a big state institution knows. This crisis is most visible in those institutions where differentiation has been carried through by mechanistic structures, systems and procedures without considering their impact on human capacities or motivation. In these types of institutions a marked loss of vitality, decreased motivation, high levels of absenteeism, and continued communication difficulties are evident.[6] While symptoms of this crisis are clearest in large bureaucracies and many companies in traditional manufacturing sectors, they also appear in smaller initiatives which have been in the differentiation phase for some time. The weight of the past, endless committee meetings, a lack of purpose and limited innovation are symptoms which become evident in well-established schools, hospitals and smaller retail companies. Being well-established and in most cases quite secure, it is as if they too were experiencing a kind of mid-life crisis, searching for new meanings and a new way of working.

The interest in co-operative and associative models, in Japanese management forms and in the qualities of excellence suggests that there is a conscious and widespread search underway in Western societies for possible answers to the crisis of differentiation.[7] The critiques of the Harvard Business

School and similar institutions, and the widespread focus on new entrepreneurship – rather than the rational model – is another manifestation of this search for a new set of organisational principles. There are as yet no definitive answers, and I believe no one organisation that offers the model for the future, but a direction and some new principles are visible.

The Integration Phase: Creating a Responsive Process Organisation

In their best-selling book, *In Search of Excellence,* Peters and Waterman point to a number of basic qualities which have made some mature American companies successful.[8] These include:

1. Clear-cut goals and a culture of commitment and excellence
2. Treating people as people and valuing their contribution
3. A decentralised and flat structure
4. An awareness of the central work processes in organisations and greater support for these processes rather than to administrative procedures and control.[9]

The findings of this book support much of the research on organisational creativity conducted since the sixties, as well as the approach developed by the member institutions of the NPI Association for Social Development.[10] Our work in many different organisations suggests that a mature institution facing a crisis of the 'administrative' or differentiation phase needs to consciously enter a new cycle in its development, opting for a new set of values, a different orientation towards work activity and simpler, decentralised structures. We believe this is as true for manufacturing companies as it is for service institutions, schools and shops which have reached maturity.

Practically, this means that a mature institution needs to formulate a new set of simple, yet meaningful goals related to the essential products or services provided to clients. These goals need to be an integral part of the organisation's past – its biography – to be authentic and to have the capacity of motivating both clients and co-workers or employees. What are a school's central educational goals and its educational philosophy, and how do they relate to the needs of both parents and students? What is a group of architects or a law firm really seeking to offer a client? Is a store or a company actually offering a set of quality products? It does not do to *say* quality or service to customers is number one if they have never been so and there is no intention of making it a reality. Implied in this effort to re-formulate goals or purposes is the recognition that people need to be able to find meaning in their work and in their lives. An organisational culture that responds to this need in an honest way gains the commitment of its people and a direction and purpose for itself.

In the differentiation phase the basic aims of a school, a hospital or a company tended to get lost over time as technical, administrative and financial concerns became paramount. The focus of attention had quite properly shifted inward to make sure that things were functioning rationally. But the price of this inward focus is a loss of connection to clients and a dimming of the vision which made the initiative what it is. As in the beginning of the differentiation phase, an entry into full and conscious maturity, into the integration phase of the organisation'a life cycle, requires renewed attention to the initiative's central tasks and goals. This can be done through a detailed study of the organisation's biography, a conscious celebration of its uniqueness and a restatement of its central goals.

Implied in this reformulation of goals is waking up to the 'sleeping partners' of the initiative, the customers and clients. The principle of association, of dialogue needs to be adopted so that the initiative really knows the needs and preferences of those it seeks to serve. A school needs an active parent council and student council so that teachers, parents, students and the community can have a frank discussion of needs and possibilities. A clinic or therapeutic centre requires a patient group, and a farm or food store a consumer circle. Only by taking such steps can the mature initiative avoid the one-sidedness of deciding by itself what an outside group needs, and keep its goals, products and services in touch with changing people and a changing culture.

A second important aspect of the integration phase is the further development of the values and criteria which go into the organisation's decision-making process. In the pioneer phase, customer satisfaction and survival was paramount, while the economic base of the initiative was being built. In the next phase of development, administrative and technical criteria played an even greater role, so that the implementation of new information systems or production systems to increase efficiency were often more important than their impact on people. In the integration phase, technical, financial and social or human criteria need to be consciously balanced. If one looks at an initiative as containing these three sub-systems, then a decision in one area has implications for the others:

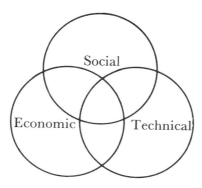

A new technical system will affect social relationships and

financial outcomes. A new product line requires investment, training, shifts in work patterns and new equipment. Consequently, any important decision needs to consider the consequences in these three areas and to include those measures or activities which will assure an integrated approach. Most importantly, the human impact of change needs to be considered and human needs taken more consciously into account in the integration phase.

A third area is related to this latter point – namely a conscious understanding of the human being as the essential ingredient in any successful initiative. Most organisations going through the differentiation phase divide the work process in such a way that some people are involved in planning and delegating work (managers), others are involved in doing it (workers), and still others in controlling it and checking it (quality control). This is, of course, most visible in large product organisations making cars, refrigerators or tubular steel. However, it is also a tendency in law firms, doctors' offices, hospitals, and other initiatives where senior members plan work, less senior people do it, and others check and control. This simple division of labour is important, yet it has the consequence of using the soul capacities of people in a one-sided way. Who has not laughed or cried at the architect who has designed an office that is uninhabitable or a house that cannot be built because the designer did not understand either offices or building materials? Equally, we have all experienced a person doing a specific job and following instructions but not being able to carry it out properly because he did not really understand how it related to a customer's need. In the first case, the architect is using the ability to think in order to design; in the second a person is using their will to do. Human beings, however, have three soul capacities: to think and plan, to will and do, and to feel and be responsible. The modern division of labour and the related high levels of specialisation foster a one-sided development of soul faculties. This tendency is particularly pronounced in the differentiation phase of an initiative. In the integration phase the three soul capacities again need to be more consciously taken into account in building semi-autonomous work or project teams, which over time acquire the quality of planning, executing and controlling their own work within general guidelines. The creation of such groups or teams requires delegation, open sharing of goals and other information, and often time and training. But without steps in this direction, people will use their ingenuity to circumvent time or quality systems, their feelings to 'rip off' the organisation and their will to build model boats at home. A culture of excellence, of commitment, means not only creating an organisation with worthwhile goals, but also one in which people have an opportunity of using their innate faculties for the benefit of the whole. A recognition of the full potential of human creativity also involves a commitment to professional development activities, flexibility in work hours and scheduling, and the fostering of individual initiative.

Self-administered initiatives in the cultural or service spheres may feel that this does not apply to them. But here too differentiation inevitably leads to the hiring of administrators, bookkeepers, secretaries, maintenance men, cooks and others. Teachers also should have an insight into the bookkeeping and the supply ordering system. The same people doing the same jobs for too many years fosters one-sidedness. The question then emerges, how can people be helped to both broaden their insights and balance the use of their capacities.

Perhaps the key element for initiative seeking to overcome the limitations of the differentiation phase is for individuals and teams to develop a new awareness of the central rhythms and work processes of the initiative, and structuring activities to facilitate these processes. In the differentiation phase the organisation was understood and viewed from a functional and hierarchical point of view. This is a vertical consciousness leading to organisation charts looking like Christmas trees with packages dangling from the boughs. In the integration phase a horizontal consciousness is in place. To put this simply, an initiative needs a purpose, a set of questions it is responding to; it requires know-how and information to respond to this need; it organises work activities to respond to the customer's or client's wants, and it does so by using financial, human, and technical resources. A school responds to the educational needs of children through a curriculum and philosophy of education, guiding a sequence of educational activities from kindergarten through a number of grades, and using a building and teachers to carry out the educational process. Visualising these activities leads to the following picture:

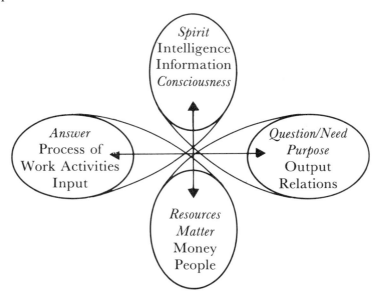

This basic sequence of responding to needs by putting human ingenuity and resources to work is, of course, present from the time the initiative begins, but it is hidden. The trick in the integration phase is to see the organisation as a process organism and to restructure it to enhance the central processes. If you think of a company from the viewpoint of the production process – inventory control, production teams, quality teams, shipping and delivery – you divide work vertically, usually blocking communication between segments while co-ordination takes place at higher management levels. The same is true of a clinic or even a self-administered school with many committees carrying out discrete functional tasks and referring to a central decision-making body for co-ordination. In the case of the company, a review of the central work process might lead to a production team having responsibility for purchasing, inventory control, quality control and shipping, as well as production. Certainly modern information systems now make it possible to contemplate such steps. The limitations are that management levels would decrease and that information would need to be shared more fully. In addition, production teams would be required to accept increased responsibility. Quality circles and job enrichment experiments have, however, indicated that such steps are not only possible but can lead to increased efficiency and greater worker satisfaction.

In self-administered schools, shops or clinics, steps in this direction are also possible – perhaps putting the functions of publicity, external relations, enrolment and fundraising into one committee, and generally simplifying the organisation's structure in line with central work processes.

As part of the new process consciousness, a new awareness of the time rhythms affecting the initiative are important. What are the sales and production cycles? What is the weekly, monthly and annual rhythm in the classroom? What is the appropriate time sequence for the budgeting and financial review process? What are the human requirements for rejuvenation and professional development?

By paying attention to this dimension of the organisation, one is beginning to build the life body of the organism. It was always there, but in the differentiation phase the qualities of leadership, of administration were central so that a kind of soul differentiation took place in the organism. In the pioneer phase, on the other hand, the initial identity and the first aspects of the physical form, of buildings and facilities, were the focus of awareness.

The consequence of a new integrated process consciousness is also simpler, decentralised and flatter structures on a human scale. Limited administration and 'lean' are current American phrases to describe these qualities of the integration phase.

When an organisation has moved toward integration, its ability to respond to its environment is enhanced, its internal functioning is more streamlined, and people can have a renewed sense of pride in their work. One could say it has achieved full maturity and a collective wisdom which also allows it to help other initiatives and to serve the wider needs of its community.

In summary, the qualities of the integration phase include:

1. Renewing central aims and the organisation's values and culture to provide meaning.
2. Creating the organs for an association – a conscious dialogue with customers, clients, suppliers and the community in which the initiative is active.
3. A leadership and decision-making style which takes human needs into account, explicitly balancing financial, technical and social criteria. Consciousness not limited to rational analysis.
4. An enhanced understanding of human beings and the creation of work processes and structures which take this new understanding of human capacities into account.
5. Creating a process organisation in which structures reflect the requirements of central work processes rather than administrative control mechanisms. Paying attention to and enhancing the rhythmic quality of the initiative's life.
6. Building teams and smaller, decentralised and flatter organisational forms.
7. Process, horizontal thinking, rather than vertical and hierarchical thinking.

These qualities do not add up to an organisational blueprint. Rather, they suggest a type of awareness, a way of looking at and understanding organisations and people from a less analytical, but deeper, more whole and conscious perspective. This perspective and the resulting direction are being explored by many initiatives today, for we all face the question of what new organisational forms are appropriate for the highly individualised consciousness we have in Western societies.

A Conscious Ending?

If the pioneer stage can be likened to childhood, the differentiation phase to early and middle adulthood, and the integration phase to full maturity and old age, what can be said about the death of an initiative? A convenient response is to say that they die when they fail and are no longer needed. However, I feel that many institutions have not only become old, but also sclerotic, disposing of vast resources but no longer really serving human needs. What would happen to cultural, social and economic creativity if institutions over one hundred years old turned over their resources to new groups wishing to respond to similar needs in new ways? What a peaceful on-going creative revolution society would experience. To do this would require institutions to contemplate a conscious death process in order to allow a new resurrection. It is an intriguing thought, if not a present reality.

The Image of Development

What has been presented is a sketch of developmental patterns in organisations. Frequently I am asked, can't a stage be missed? The answer is no if organisations have a true life cycle moving from simple to more complex, from one central organising principle to another. This means that true development is a discontinuous, irreversible process in time, moving from a stage of growth through differentiation to a higher stage of integration and passing through states of crisis which offer the impetus for development. This pattern is, I believe, true for all living forms, for the human being, and for organisations.

However, it is possible for initiatives to move more or less rapidly through these phases. A school which starts with six grades and a kindergarten will face questions of differentiation sooner than one which starts with one grade, adding a new grade each year. A company which has twenty employees the first year and four hundred the second will also face developmental issues more rapidly than one which grows more slowly. Furthermore, it is quite common for large organisations to have different segments at different stages of development. A new product division may be in the pioneer stage, the mother company may be going through the crisis of differentiation, while one older division may already have started working with the principles of integration.

In presenting this picture of organisation development, a number of complementary images have been alluded to. They can be summarised as follows and require some further explanation:

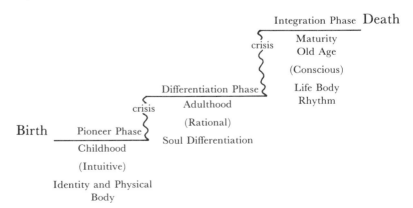

The image of birth, childhood, adulthood, maturity and death is a metaphor which is quite clear. The words intuitive, rational and conscious can be used to describe the dominant soul states (or types of consciousness) in different phases of an initiative's life.[11] The reference to the Ego and physical form in the pioneer stage, Soul differentiation in the differentiation phase, and Life Body in the integration phase indicates that organisation development is a human creation process in which human beings can more and more consciously develop the sheaths or the vessel in which the spirit of the initiative can live. While these sheaths are present from the beginning, their enhancement and unfolding requires conscious human activity, focusing first on identity and growth, then on soul differentiation, and lastly on the rhythmic life body of the initiative.

The described image of an initiative's development over time is incomplete. Like all ideal-type descriptions it cannot do justice to the rich texture of organisational life, nor to the uniqueness of each initiative.[12] Its purpose is rather to describe a landscape of possibilities, indicating paths to be pursued and pitfalls to be avoided so that we may become more conscious and responsible co-creators on earth.

Exercise: The Developing Organisation

The concept of the developing organisation can be used as a diagnostic tool to enable one to become clearer about the stage of development in which the organisation, one's own department and one's personal style fits.

1. At what stage is the organisation now? What are the characteristics of the prevailing structure

Continued

and 'climate'? In which areas is there still a pioneer style, or remnants of it? Where is it a rational organisation and where can one already find elements of integrated organisation? Where are there transitions?

2. What is the situation in respect to your department? Is it at the beginning, in the middle, or at the end of the rational phase, or already into the integrated phase? What is the history of your department in this organisation?

3. What are your own views and intentions: Do you like to go into action quickly on the basis of a concrete question, do you prefer to organise well prepared activities according to plan, or is the more integrated approach more satisfying to you? And what about your colleagues?

4. What questions arise within you as a result of this diagnosis of the future of organisation?

Case Study: Townsend and Bottum Inc. – Continuity Planning and a New Ownership Form[13]

Bill Bottum is a thoughtful and gregarious man in his late fifties. He had joined Townsend and Bottum as a young engineer when the organisation was led by his father. By 1979 he had been the chief executive officer for some time. The company was facing a changing market in the construction industry and he was aware that new strategies, a new ownership form and succession planning were required if

Townsend and Bottum were to successfully enter the 1980's. In March 1979 he called together the top managers of the company for a long term strategic planning meeting. The results of this meeting were to be dramatic over the next five years, leading to a process of change in the company's direction, in relationships, in structure and in the form of ownership.

Seen from the outside, this change process in Townsend and Bottum comprised five main areas. One was the focusing of the company's mission and values – or its corporate culture. Townsend and Bottum in 1985 developed a T. and B. Mission statement which stressed serving the real needs of clients with absolute integrity. It also noted that the values within the organisation were to be commensurate with the tenets of the world's great religions, and that the organisation and its employees were to be 'a witness, an example, of human and spiritual values to employees, clients, business and community'.

A second area of change was in the quality of relationships.[1] The company's objective was to 'create a climate of openness, sincerity, integrity and trust' capable of permeating the organisation and its internal and external relationships. The company took a number of steps toward this objective, beginning in 1974 with communication skills training. Status symbols separating employees were removed. Over one hundred employees took part in team building and communication workshops designed and carried out by an external consulting firm. Team building and conflict resolution workshops were also extended to relationships with client organisations so that joint problem solving orientations were fostered. The concept of leadership was examined and use was made of Robert K. Greenleaf's book *Servant Leadership – A Journey into the Nature of Legitimate Power and Greatness*. Greenleaf stresses that effective leaders of the future will be motivated by a desire to serve rather than a drive for power and status. In addition, employees were encouraged to reflect on their own styles of working, through using a Life Styles Inventory, developed by Human Synergistics in Plymouth, Michigan. The idea of being an effective model rather than a moraliser was central to the process of creating greater trust and co-operation within the organisation.

A third area of development was the restructuring and decentralisation of the company. In 1978 T. and B. consisted of one main company, Townsend and Bottum with 664 employees, Project Management Associates with 31 employees and Jilco Inc. with 28 employees. By 1985 it consisted of fourteen decentralised groups including the 'not for profit' Servant Leader Centre as the research and educational component of T. and B.

The fourth area of major change was finding an ownership form which would guarantee the continuity of the company. After much research a Capital Fund form was chosen. This meant that private share-holders were bought out and that a Board of Trustees would hold the company's assets for the company's present and future employees.

A last question for the organisation was passing the reins of responsibility to a new generation of managers. This process is still under-way with Bill Bottum having resigned as chief executive officer and functioning as a mentor and advisor to the new top management team.

The Townsend Bottum experience, described in outline form, is beginning to serve as an inspiration to other businesses who seek to become more service oriented, human, moral and effective modern industries. It is a heart-warming effort to bring new values and forms into economic life. A summary of key concepts is added.

For more information write to: The Servant Leader Centre, 2245 South State Street, P.O. Box 1368, Ann Arbor, MI 48106, U.S.A.

SOME KEY CONCEPTS

1. Neutralisation of Capital – Capital is a working tool for each generation of managers.

2. Portion of increases in capital goes to current managers. Balance accumulates.

3. Recognise individual differences in talent, capability, and business judgement.

4. Co-operation and brotherhood in economic sphere.

5. Equality in rights sphere.

6. Liberty and freedom in spiritual activity – encourage growth and development.

7. Self-transcending motivation toward benefit for all mankind.

FUTURE:

8. Producer's income diminishes when losses occur, thus stabilising employment.

ADDRESSED BY

1. Continuity Plan which eliminates common stock. Governance by Trustees.

2. Income Distribution Units (I.D.U.) Programme shares profits – bonus pool.

3. Compensation and I.D.U. Systems reward performance. Trustees not elected.

4. Team-Building programmes including clients. Communication skill training.

5. Equal opportunity. Eliminate status symbols. Participative management.

6. By-Laws provide for religious freedom. Life Styles Inventory for development.

7. Servant Leader Centre. Guiding principles.

FUTURE:

8. A. Spun off entities self-adjust pay to respond to market.

   B. Explore application to T&B Family of Companies.

Chapter Seven

Initiatives and Individual Development

Christopher Schaefer

Developing New Capacities

The word initiative comes from initiation, a process of inner transformation leading to spiritual enlightenment. Such a connection may seem grand to us today and yet it does point to the truth that there is an intimate relationship between the strengths and weaknesses of an initiative and the strengths and weaknesses of the founding or carrying personalities. The store with irregular hours, the printing business that commits repeated mistakes or the school which is always messy reveals something about the personality characteristics of the carrying individuals. The changes in the fortunes of an initiative can often be dramatic when this relation between the enterprise and the carrying person or group is made visible and when a change in attitude or behaviour results; in short, when individual development takes place.

The close relation between ourselves and the initiatives we are involved with raises the question of how we can more consciously address the individual development opportunities inherent in our working life. The following discussion indicates avenues of exploration, suggesting areas for learning and inner work.

The process of initiative-taking has already been described in some detail. If one looks at what is implied, then one can say that initiative-takers require the ability to perceive what is needed, respond with confidence and flexibility to this need, and possess both courage and persistence. This is a tall order, and yet these qualities are repeatedly tested in the early years of an enterprise.

Is the perceived need real or an individual pipe dream? Only the response of the public will tell. I remember sitting in an office in late spring mailing the brochures of a new social training course to many parts of the world and having the sinking thought, perhaps no one will want to come.

Even if the need is real, the ability to respond to it requires great inner flexibility, not to speak of long hours and sacrifice. Temporary buildings, a different location, part-time outside work or a modification of product or service may be required. A compromise with reality, with the earth, is asked for and this sorely tests our resolve. A training centre for young people, which was intended for a rural setting, ended up in the centre of a small English city; a Waldorf school wished for spacious pleasant surroundings, but had to rent ugly antiquated premises in Chicago; and a recently started café in Detroit ended up next to an old bar and near an adult (blue) movie theatre. These steps required compromise, a modification of expectations, but they made life possible.

The qualities of courage and persistence are equally vital. The initiative begins with nothing except an idea and perhaps some friends. So in taking an initiative we are going into the unknown with only ourselves as resources. Subconsciously and sometimes consciously we feel that we may fail and be exposed to ridicule or criticism. So a threshold of fear needs to be crossed, not only once but repeatedly. In other cases the fear of success may play in. If we succeed, then we have to take ourselves seriously and be responsible. I believe that fear of failure or success is the cause for many unborn initiatives and for many which die in infancy. But if we dare and start and continue, then we acquire, use, and build courage.

In addition to courage, the 'long will' is needed – the quality of perseverance. We have the saying, 'Rome was not built in a day,' indicating that patience and a long term commitment is needed to realise an aim. Fortunately, we are not able to see all the obstacles which the initiative will encounter in its life before we start, otherwise we probably would never begin.

The points mentioned are, I believe, obvious for anyone who has ever been involved in starting something. As is frequently pointed out, initiatives 'build character'. By stepping back and reflecting on our experiences we can see that initiatives are a potential training ground for our faculties of soul, in particular the qualities of thinking, feeling and willing. Thought and perception are crucial in seeing and having the right thinking response to a need; a balance in our feeling life is vital if the ups and downs of the initiative process are not to create inner havoc; and a mastery of will is required for the long pull of creating and developing the initiative. Thus taking initiatives strengthens and develops our individual soul capacities.[1]

This development can be further enhanced through inner exercises, as for example, the six subsidiary exercises described by Rudolf Steiner. These exercises develop the control of thinking; of action; of composure or equanimity; positivity; an open mind and a balanced, all round personal development. (See Box overleaf.)

Exercises for Self-Development

The six exercises are as follows and are to be practiced sequentially, adding later ones when familiarity has been achieved with earlier ones.

1) *The Mastery of Thought Life:*
   The individual is asked to determine the sequence of his or her thoughts by focusing attention on simple objects, such as the origin, function and make-up of a paper clip, a pencil or a candle. By practising this daily, the tendency to wander in one's thoughts, and to have unrealistic conceptions, can be overcome so that thoughts will more reflect inner effort and have a relation to external fact.

2) *The Mastery over Will Impulses:*
   Rarely do will impulses originate in conscious intentions. Rudolf Steiner therefore suggests giving oneself a small but conscious task at a given point during the day – for example, retying a shoelace at 4 p.m., or observing a plant at 1 p.m.. What matters is the exactitude with which we accomplish such tasks, adding more and more consciousness to our will life.

3) *Equanimity in our Feeling Life:*
   This exercise can be repeatedly practised and is not directed at suppressing feelings, but rather at not letting feelings dominate one's life and reactions. Moments of joy and sorrow are part of life, but often they overtake us, leading to

Continued

excessive actions or moods. The point is to maintain some inner composure within the vicissitudes of life.

4) *Positivity in Judgements about People and the World:*
We are often confronted with life situations where judgements are made about the quality of work done, tardiness at meetings, or an argument between colleagues. This exercise suggests reviewing such situations and seeing people and life in a broader context. A person may be habitually late, but a closer look reveals that he is always responding to other people's needs. An accident is not only hurtful but may lead to something important and new in life. We have the opportunity of practising a conscious positivity and understanding many times a day, thereby avoiding getting into fixed and often negative positions. Work with this exercise leads to openness in an individual and the ability to experience aspects of life previously missed.

5) *Lack of Preconceptions or Openness in Understanding Life:*
Here it is suggested that we practise being open to that which is new; a different opinion, a new person, an unusual request, or a new way of developing one's initiative.

6) *The harmonious balance between these attributes:*
The six exercises should not be developed in a one-sided way, and it is for that reason that it is suggested doing just one every day for a month

Continued

and then moving on to a second, a third and so on; or adding a second one the second month until all six are being worked with.[2] The reason for balance is obvious insofar as the first three focus on thinking, willing and feeling respectively, while four and five have more to do with attitudes linking different soul attributes, and six is a kind of call for review and balance.

The exercises may appear both simple and somewhat contrived. By doing them it will be observed that far from being easy, they demand repeated effort. I can attest to their difficulty. As to being stilted, it is best to try them and see what effects they have on your outer and inner life. Such a trial will, I believe, indicate their central relevance to taking initiatives as they reinforce the learning which our working lives continuously confront us with.

Moments of Self Reflection

In looking at the conscious development of the initiatives, the importance of stepping back from the pressures of the everyday and reviewing what has happened in the past and what is wanted for the future was repeatedly stressed. This periodic extended review and planning time involves developing an objective picture of the initiative's biography, its past strengths and weaknesses, and formulating a joint and consciously-willed picture of the future. Behind such a suggestion is the idea that we learn most by consciously reviewing and digesting our experiences and then projecting the lessons learned forward.

While engaging in such periodic reflections about the initiative, we can become much more aware of our role in it and how our personality affects it. While reviewing the functioning of an institution I was involved with in England, I noticed that one of its areas of weakness was that it paid little attention to administrative practices and that it had limited rhythm and regularity in its staff and administrative meetings. On further reflection, I became aware of my own desk, my dislike of paperwork, and my interest in new meetings and projects. The connection seemed to be more than coincidental, and I was forced to work with it. Indeed I have found the connection between the character of an initiative and the strengths and weaknesses of the founding personalities to be so striking that often just creating an awareness of it will lead to substantial individual and institutional change.

Such moments of reflection in the life of the initiative can clearly bring greater individual self-knowledge as well as being essential to the healthy development of the venture. We can consciously extend this principle to the rest of our lives by choosing to create periods of quiet reflection. In so doing, we are meeting one of the conditions of inner development – creating moments of inner tranquillity – in which we have the possibility of distinguishing the essential from the nonessential in our lives. Rudolf Steiner suggests that 'our aim in these moments of seclusion must be so to contemplate and judge our actions and experiences as though they applied not to ourselves but to some other person.' Through such a practice in our initiatives and in our lives we gain greater understanding and increase our strength to serve moral human goals.

Working with Others as an Aspect of Individual Development

Many newly created institutions embody the ideals of working together for worthwhile aims. A measure of equality is often sought and aspects of mutual interdependence are acknowledged. And yet it often appears to be so hard to work together, to achieve agreement and to create a positive collegial environment. One of the reasons for this is that we all naturally possess strong self-centred anti-social qualities, as was discussed previously.

If we focus on the mirroring, balancing function which working relationships provide for us, then one of the most obvious is bringing our self-interested anti-social side to awareness. If we pay careful attention to our thought life when listening to another, we can notice that we selectively listen to what we agree or disagree with and then busily formulate a response. Observed more closely, we can see the quality of doubt, of critical intelligence directed at the thoughts of others.

If we observe our feelings, we can notice that our relationships are coloured by a sea of sympathies and antipathies. There are some people in a working group whom I naturally like, agree with, and enjoy, and others with whom I have difficulty, no matter what they do. These likes and dislikes are not only the basis for judgements about others, but often also the basis of far-reaching decisions. Yet such feelings are usually quite unreliable, as they tend to say more about what we like or don't like about ourselves than anything objective about the other. These natural likes and dislikes can be the greatest enemies of true social life since they often block the development of real interest between people, hindering the search for a deeper, conscious understanding of human relationships.[3] The picture which has sometimes come to my mind regarding these forces of sympathy and antipathy is that they give rise to a butterfly collector mentality in us – they tempt us to categorise and then pin people to particular images. Once done, it is impossible for anyone to escape – 'Tom is always late, isn't he?' – and we needn't actually concern ourselves with individuals any more. They are, after all, already categorised in our private collection.

If we observe our behaviour, our intentions, something of our will in a group, we can quickly notice that when we get our way we are pleased, gracious, even open, but when we do not we react in a variety of negative ways. At this more subtle and less conscious level of the soul a certain selfishness and egotism reigns, even when couched in terms of wanting what is good for others or for the community. Marjorie Spock discusses this issue at some length in her important article, *Reflections on Community Building.*

Through working with others we can come to recognise three fundamental anti-social forces in our soul:

- Doubt and criticism in our thought life.
- Sympathy and antipathy in our feeling life.
- Egotism and selfishness in our will life.

While these three soul forces lead us to greater self-consciousness, they can also block a genuine meeting with others.

Knowing about our anti-social nature is of course not adequate – it must be repeatedly experienced and ultimately *accepted* if we are even to consider a future transformation. For this to happen it is not only important that individuals review their daily experiences, but that groups and institutions review their meetings and the quality of their working relationships. Only through a review process of meetings and decisions can we begin to remind each other what we have achieved and not achieved, recall our anti-social nature, and gradually build that loyalty and caring which makes mutual development possible.

A second balancing factor to be experienced in our new living and working arrangements is a growing individual awareness of our untransformed sides. Jung refers to this as the 'shadow' and Rudolf Steiner as the 'double'.[5] Especially in conflict situations we can notice that suddenly we are consumed by anger, or hatred. In some people this appears primarily as heat, as a violent mood which arises within, overwhelming all common sense. In others, there may be a cold, manipulative hatred which seeks to inflict pain. Often both qualities are present. In this experience we see something of the faces of evil. To acknowledge the presence of such qualities as 'mine', as requiring transformation and inner development, is to begin to take spiritual beings – including ourselves – seriously.

So far, we have concentrated on how human relationships and working groups can provide balance through making us aware of our anti-social nature, and of our untransformed 'double'. This reflecting, mirror function is an essential service we can do for each other, no matter how badly or semi-consciously. It is something for which we need to learn gratitude, although it can be a most jarring experience.

The mirror function of working groups and of conscious relationships can be seen as a call to see ourselves more clearly and to develop. Fortunately another quality is present when we live and work with each other over time – an invitation to develop interest, understanding, and ultimately the beginnings of love. This invitation is subtle and only becomes apparent over time.We may notice that a particular person always brings the discussion back to a point that we left ten minutes ago. At first this is annoying, perhaps even maddening, but then one day we notice the important clarifications that result. We become interested, we listen to how the person expresses his or her thoughts, how this annoying quality can work positively, as well as negatively. The spark of initial interest is a door through which we can proceed. We may ask what temperament, what background, what life history expresses itself in this person? In short, we seek some understanding of the other. The more we learn the more we appreciate how different people are, how fundamentally other is their experience of the world. This process can lead to a friendship and to the thought, 'How wonderful that they are different – that there are differences between people.' Perhaps some weeks or months later when we are facing an important decision in the group, the same person again brings up an issue left behind long ago, this time negatively so that others react badly. The resulting injury to that person leads us to act. After the meeting we go to the person, we discuss it and share some of our observations, not out of anger, but out of understanding and compassion.

We all have experiences of this kind but perhaps don't realise their importance. Initially, when we begin to listen we are turning our thought consciousness outward – turning doubt into interest – moving from a closed gesture to an open one. This turning of thought into active listening – into interest – requires effort. It is a willing-thinking listening process. Once accomplished, it often activates our feeling toward the other, transforming our natural sympathies and antipathies into an organ of perception, into a feeling understanding, and objective empathy. In so doing we replace the natural sympathies and antipathies with understanding. This is important in social life, for the butterfly collection in our soul is a kind of coffin for others, making them unfree. To rid ourselves of fixed images of others, to develop a picture based on warm understanding, carrying in it a recognition of their striving spirit – and of that which they are struggling to transform – is a vital social deed.

A warm and objective understanding of another in our feeling life can then also fire the will, transforming egotistic impulses into deeds of compassion and ultimately of love.

The 'mirror' and 'invitation' functions of working with others in connection with individual development can be summarised in the following manner:- (See overleaf.)

	The Mirror			The Invitation	
Awareness	Doubt	thinking	Interest	Development	
of				of	
Anti-Social	Sympathies and Antipathies	feeling	Understanding	Social	
Forces	Egotism	willing	Compassion	Forces	
	The Double			The Ego	

As experiences, the mirror and the invitation are not sequential. Sometimes genuine interest in another can make us aware that we have in the past not listened, but have met their thoughts with doubt. Sometimes it is the other way around; the awareness of our anti-social side creates a mood of humility which leads to genuine interest.

In looking at this process it is important to recognise a basic polarity which Steiner describes as the fundamental phenomenon of all social life. In meeting others we are as it were oscillating between being awake in ourselves, formulating responses, attending to our feelings – the anti-social forces; and falling asleep into others, listening to them and living into their reality – the social forces. This swing between waking to ourselves and sleeping into others is natural and can be observed in every conversation we have. To develop new social forces our ego must be strong enough to maintain consciousness while listening to and understanding others. As in all inner development, this requires a continuous and conscious struggle. A small indication of this struggle is the experience of how tiring it is to truly listen to another person for a period of time – and how enlivening to listen to oneself. I think that the practice of maintaining consciousness while using one's soul faculties of thinking, feeling and willing to understand the other is analogous to maintaining consciousness in sense-free meditation.

This is mainly because in consciously seeing the other we are perceiving the other's ego, his or her spiritual essence and force. It is this ego force which normally lulls us into semi-consciousness and which arouses the anti-social forces in us as a form of self-protection. To develop conscious social qualities is to be able to maintain consciousness in the spiritual presence of the other. This is difficult and requires ego strength. It is also a form of spiritual cognition.

The task for developing conscious social qualities is important for the individual, for others, and for initiatives. For the individual its fundamental importance lies in the fact that such a development occurs only as the individual assumes some control and mastery in his or her soul. As long as we are thought, felt and willed – pushed like a reed by the turbulence of our soul moods – true interest and understanding of others is not possible. So in becoming aware of our anti-social natures, in gaining glimpses of our double and in attempting to develop interest, understanding and compassion for others, we are on the road to attaining mastery in our soul.

Its importance for others, for social relationships, can be experienced daily. Who has not had at least one experience of being truly listened to and felt the warmth, enjoyed the resulting clarity of thought, and experienced the wonder of a true conversation. At still another level, to live and work with others who carry a true picture of ourself is to be continuously encouraged in the struggles of life. Perhaps most importantly, groups of people who are striving to develop conscious social qualities have the possibility of helping to fulfil each other's destiny. The anti-social qualities block a recognition of true human possibilities. More conscious social qualities and relationships create an open space in which individual strengths, weaknesses and potentials can be mutually worked with.

For groups and initiatives seeking to serve the needs of the time, the individual development of new social faculties is the leaven which makes such service possible. The essential relationship between the phases of an organisation's development and the type of consciousness required in the pioneer, differentiation and integration phases has already been discussed.[6] The more fundamental connection between the aims and morality of the initiative and the aims, morality and social awareness of the initiative-takers is evident upon reflection. We cannot serve positive aims or goals in freedom without a substantial measure of self-awareness and social understanding.[7]

Development in Life

I have tried to suggest that consciously taking initiatives implies a process of individual development. The aspects of such development include exercising new soul faculties, achieving moments of inner quiet, recognising our anti-social nature and developing a new understanding of others. This is a process of development in life as the opportunities for greater self-awareness and self-transformation are given to us every day. Yet it is not automatic for we need to consciously recognise that we are on the road with others and be willing to work with and share the challenges along the way. Individual development in and through life is different though connected to a conscious inner path of meditative work. The one focuses on understanding our life experiences and gradually transforming ourselves as a result in order to become a better, more conscious human being. The other usually involves working with a meditative content that is not based on sense experience in order to gradually unfold organs of spiritual cognition. A conscious choice to work with true meditative disciplines will enhance our learning in life if our motive remains one of serving the needs of the earth and of others.[8]

Chapter Eight

New Values and New Initiatives
Signs of Hope

Tijno Voors

At present we see many signs of deep human distress, but also glimpses of an awakening to new values. In what follows, we will look at some examples of the many encouraging initiatives that are taken. The examples are chosen because of their clear direction and experience. They could help to enliven our imagination if we want to take an initiative ourselves.

A Therapeutic Community for Drugtakers

One of the distressing symptoms of our time is the fact that so many people are out of work for a long time, or homeless, while others have become totally dependent on drugs or alcohol. Many have as a result of this lost all sense of identity, all sense for real life. We can also observe that increasingly people engage themselves in a variety of ways to meet and help these problems. Successful initiatives in this realm often form communities that initially serve as a refuge. These life and/or work communities gradually become a home in which people can reconnect with themselves and develop confidence to meet and engage with the world.

One such initiative is the life and work-community, ARTA, in Zeist, Holland.[1] When ARTA started in 1976, a group of people had already been working for a long time to develop a therapeutic programme for ex-drug-takers. From 1981 they developed their present programme that leads the ex-drug-takers through a process of four phases, which serve as a repetition of the phases of childhood.[2]

In so doing, the disturbances in the normal development of childhood can be corrected by the person himself, and this opens the way to finding one's individual life aims and direction.

The first phase starts on a farm. Old habits and life-style are exchanged for a rhythmic structure of the day. Everyone – co-workers and participants – engages in the daily farm life, the care of the animals, the garden and the house, and the preparation of the meals.

The second phase starts when people can live without the drugs, and a new life rhythm is found. In this phase new life-forces must be built up. Central to this is rhythm and work. Morning and late afternoon for work in the garden, wood workshop, weavery or house and kitchen. In the afternoon, participants are engaged in different medical therapies to build up their vitality. Evenings are filled with biographical conversations, and the telling of myths and legends.

The third phase is an intensification of this programme, aimed towards the discovery of one's own strengths and weaknesses. In work, participants are asked to take more responsibility – meals must be served on time, tools must be clean, workshops ready for the next day. The afternoons are filled with different artistic therapies, such as painting, drawing, modelling, massage, etc.. Participants are also invited to start studying to awaken their interest and challenge their thinking and individual judgement. The evenings are spent on topical social questions, drama, and prepared talks and evaluation.

In the fourth phase, work-and-study-programmes are gradually exchanged for placement periods in companies or institutions, or for a vocational training. The participant is somewhat more free to arrange his time, but becomes at the same time responsible for an area of work. Weekends are spent on nature walks, visiting museums or going to a theatre. Participants of the fourth phase are responsible for such weekend programmes.

Gradually the participant finds his direction and the confidence to leave ARTA. This can take place when a healthy place to live has been found, and a meaningful work or training established.

Around this programme, carried by the therapeutic community, the co-workers have developed a social and spiritual community to enable them to gain support for each other and to nurture the impulse they want to serve. The social community organises itself through the mandate-principle described in chapter three.

ARTA can be seen as one of these initiatives that work out of a deep care and respect for the individual. Moreover, they find their source of inspiration in an ever deepening understanding of the nature of the human being.

Similar initiatives have started in Germany, Sweden and the U.S.A..

Young People and Work – Streetwise yet Asleep

Other people are meeting the needs of the unemployed. One of them is Shire Training Workshops in Stroud, England. A co-worker described the life of a trainee, called Steven, as follows:

> 'Steven left school unable to read and write without great difficulty and with no ambition and

no particular hope for the future. He came to Shire Training Workshops on the recommendation of a friend who had been with us.

In the images Steven has carried of his childhood, as he told them during conversations we have had together, nothing of any beauty or magic or mystery emerges – that he can remember anyway. His experience of life thus far has been dominated by pressure from school, parents, the social system, and his inarticulate desire to get away from it. Little of harmony or vitality or eagerness seem to be reflected in what he has become. He knows much of failure, of sexual prejudice, of the system and cynicism, of the value of money. He is street-wise yet asleep.

While he is with us, Steven will go through a twelve month educational programme. He will learn how to mend a tap and how to measure a piece of wood and saw it straight. He can learn how to mix mortar and lay a brick and how to use a spirit-level. He can learn how to make pastry and soup and chocolate sponge. He will have a go at metal-work and welding and at typing, filing and answering the telephone. He will help to produce an S.T.W. trainee newsletter.

Some of these basic skills will become useful to Steven in other aspects of the programme. Working with a group of trainees and a group leader member of staff, he will go out into the community on project work: redecorating a church, renovating a children's adventure playground. He will help plan, prepare, cook and serve lunch for seventy five old age pensioners.

All the work Steven does is assessed each week and reviewed and revised at the end of each three month phase, according to our understanding of his needs. He may need help with personal problems, so there is a counsellor available to talk to. All his needs and questions, and the progress and development he makes, are discussed both with him and among the staff group.

Running through the programme are opportunities built into the working week to attempt wood-carving, stone-masonry, wet-paper painting, photography, calligraphy and other arts and crafts. These sessions are led by people who are craftsmen and, as important, teachers.

Steven will go on a residential experience for two weeks. In a distant and different place from Stroud, he will learn how it is to live and work in a community, taking part in a domestic work routine as well as a work project. Among possible activities outside this work will be pony-trekking, hill-walking and swimming.

A social and life skills programme will take Steven through a number of courses including a communications course, a course on relationships and, in the final phase, a leavers' course.

Throughout the whole of his work at Shire Training Workshops, Steven will be in constant contact with adults both within and without the staff group. And whether it is a session on wallpapering, or out digging an old age pensioner's garden, or even on a walk along the river Wye, he will be encouraged to consciously meet people both in what they can give him and what he can give them.

In socio-economic terms, the significant thing about most of the young people who come to S.T.W. is that they are superfluous to, or at least ill-equipped to fit into, the machinery of human requirements. To bring some shift in a young person from this unconscious (or conscious) identity of himself towards a sense of his worth and purpose is a difficult and sometimes disillusioning undertaking. As a staff group we have spent this first year of the Youth Training Scheme programme trying to bring to it the kind of life which will make S.T.W. less of a last resort for an unemployed school-leaver and more of an encouragement and challenge to a real young person.

What I can now say about Steven is that through the work he is encountering at S.T.W. he has begun to discover possibilities within himself. He has discovered that painting colours on white paper is not childish; that he can become absorbed by this activity for forty five minutes – probably the longest period of time he has ever been absorbed by anything. He has learnt that creativity can be good fun. Steven has overcome his fear and dislike of old and disabled people by having worked for them and with them. Steven has helped rebuild a dry-stone wall and found himself able and enthusiastic. He knows how to use a spirit-level – the result of a learning process which took some three weeks. Steven has shown that he is extremely gifted with small children; endlessly patient and willing, he knows what they enjoy doing and is happy to join in. Suddenly in this he becomes responsible, for them and for himself, awake and imaginative. Steven can see some of the work he has achieved in the short time he has been with us and knows that it is good and that he has done it. And for all that his problems have not faded away and that he is still Steven with an uncertain future, the seeds of a real hope have been sown.'

Lifeways

Another symptom of human distress is becoming visible in the last fifteen to twenty years. The life of more and more people is ruled by anxiety, insecurity and fear. Even many people who have built around themselves outer security, possessions or status, experience a sense of uneasiness or inner insecurity and fear. Many cannot sleep, are overworked, nervous, cannot cope with their relationships, feel lonely, deserted, unable to connect with others and themselves. Many people are affected by the pace of life. Demands, pressures, multitudes of impressions seem to invade them. They feel lost and for many the only way out is in taking tranquillisers or other medical treatment. What is going on?

Bernard Lievegoed describes in his book *'Man on the Threshold'*[3] that humanity is more and more faced with forces of his own inner world. He writes: 'Instead of voyages of discovery to unknown continents, as took place at the beginning of the New Age, one now has to explore unknown territories in one's own human psyche'. Many people are not prepared for what they meet, they get lost, get out of breath, and find it difficult to keep a certain rhythm in their daily life. An increasing need is expressed to regain a connection with the practice of daily life. This was very strongly confirmed through the success of the book *'Lifeways'*[4] edited by Gudrun Davy and Bons Voors. This book is about children, about family life, about being a parent, but most of all about the tension between personal fulfilment and domestic obligation. It is a book written by mothers and fathers, about 'coping alone', 'festivals', 'family meals', 'role exchange', 'illness', 'living in time' and much more. They write out of their own experience about lifeways that can support all those involved. A reader, mother from the U.S.A. with three children wrote:

'I am from a working class background. My mother worked and so did her mother. I have three small children, and I do not know where or how to start to build a family life at home. I have chosen to be a mother, and, boy, it's the hardest job I've ever taken on. I am just about drowning, but I am still determined to become a good mother and a good wife. The book *Lifeways* is my lifebelt. I underline things which I find helpful. I realise I am not the only one who finds it difficult. I am reading all these wonderful suggestions and ways to look at things. Last Christmas was the first time we made things instead of buying presents. It was very special.'

A book can help, but many people are searching for places where they can meet, where they can be themselves or engage themselves in activities that are meaningful for them. Such places could be called *Life-Centres* because they will help people to reconnect with life.

Life-Centres – Forum 3

Forum 3 in Stuttgart, West Germany, is one of these places. Forum 3[5] started in 1969 at the time of the Prague-Spring. A small group of architects, actors and craftsmen realised there was a need for a meeting-place, a Forum. The place became known and gathered many young people who felt there was a sympathetic ear for their ideas and problems. Activities developed and at present the 'tea-rooms' are a central meeting place for 4,000 to 5,000 people each month. Many activities take place, such as music, theatre groups, production of a newsletter, preparation for festivals, peace groups, study groups, arts and craft activities. The clown, Nögge, devotes much time to creating the type of entertainment that raises important social questions and issues of our time. In addition, there are many visitors who take part in repairing the fabric of the house and other such activities. By working together in this, way with the co-workers, warmth and openness is created, and through this it is easier to communicate inner thoughts and thereby initiate real dialogue and recognition. Since it is mainly for young people, discussion tends to centre upon issues which affect them such as mis-information and lack of understanding of drugs, spiritual movements, problems of housing and accommodation, peace, East-West relations, and so on.

The secret of the place lies in the ability of the co-workers to listen to the people and not tell them what they should do. They say: 'Listening helps to awaken the spirit that lives in every person'.

From the beginning of Forum 3 it was also felt that in order to understand and meet people where they are, Forum 3 had to have an open relationship with many kinds of people, political parties and causes. On the other hand, it also believes that along with other characteristic emphases, such as non-violence, it must have its own firm spiritual identity. From out of this it makes its dialogue and environment.

It has also chosen a structure that supports the three-fold nature of the human being, that is to say, the will within people's actions, the feelings between people, and the life of thoughts. In Forum 3 they firmly believe that without an inner and outer structure for people's activities, people become ill and confused, for they have no landmarks with which to find their way.

In recent years, many more places like Forum 3 are springing up. Many opportunities for new initiatives are waiting, before every town has its own Life-Centre.

A Community Farm

Another area of great concern to many people is related to the exploitation of the earth and the quality of food that is consumed by many millions of people. Organic and Bio-dynamic farms are experiencing the demand of a rapidly growing market for wholefood products. The price to acquire farmland, however, makes it virtually impossible to buy and develop a farm according to organic or bio-dynamic principles.

This was clearly demonstrated in the development of Old

Plaw Hatch Farm in Sharpthorne, England. This farm, since 1970 farmed on bio-dynamic principles, was privately owned and supplied the local community with unpasteurised milk. The capitalisation and running of the farm was a continuous struggle, and in 1980 the farm was offered for sale.

A local land trust, already owning some farmland, was asked to acquire the land on behalf of the community. At a public meeting, consumers, living in the local community, were asked to buy the farm. The community responded beyond expectation and gifts of over £50,000 were promised. This positive response made it possible for the Trustees to acquire low interest loans through Mercury Provident Society and its sister bank in Germany. They were able to lend a total of £100,000 for a lower interest.

A separate company was formed for the farming activity, the shares of which were held by the same land trust, and the two farmers responsible for the farm were appointed directors of the Company. A sum of £32,000 was needed to purchase the live and dead stock of the farm, and Mercury and the German bank were able to make this loan. In order to demonstrate the support of the local community, personal guarantees from members of the community were required to cover at least half of the amount.

Within three years of purchase, the Trust received covenants and legacies which enabled it to pay off the greater part of its loan and to carry out substantial improvements to land and buildings. The milk round of unpasteurised milk continues to flourish and a Government sponsored scheme, using local unemployed young people, has opened up neglected areas on the farm to the public for recreational purposes.

The farm, now owned by the local community through the Landtrust, stands in a unique position to involve the community in many activities on the farm such as festivals, harvesting and providing a place for the local schools to further the pupils' understanding of nature and agriculture. But the primary gift of the community and others was to remove the land from the property market and make it freely available for the development of bio-dynamic farming.

New Directions in Economic Life

Finally we should look at the realities of working life in organisations. Many organisations have increasingly become systemised, large scale and bureaucratic.

The triumph of technical science in this century, and especially the effects of automation, have robbed many people of a chance to engage creatively in their work. Work has lost its meaning. Money seems the only motivation for many to be at work.

Many organisations, and now also countries, are in debt. Huge sums of money are pushed like a grey cloud over the globe, giving speculators a great time, but keeping the world monetary system in a constant state of emergency. What is really happening? People feel at a loss. Many people give up. Others, however, yearn for understanding. Why should everything be so big, so impersonal, so void of human values? They call for organisations on a human scale, in which people can relate to what they are doing and can engage themselves with each other. They call for new social forms that challenge people to participate, because they have had enough of being a cog in the machine. They are interested in new ways of financing their business, new approaches to salaries, new ways of influencing the flow of money in the organisation. They are searching for a new social understanding and an insight into the spiritual nature of the world.

New initiatives are becoming visible, that are addressing these questions. The Other Economic Summit (TOES), established in 1984, ran at the same time as the London Economic Summit of the Heads of State of the seven richest Western countries. Many other initiatives are searching for new understanding and workable alternatives.

Many inspiring examples of alternative agriculture, work-ers participation, co-operatives and community initiatives, in

Britain, the U.S.A. and Canada, as well as in many of the Developing Countries, are described in the book *'Small is Possible'* by George McRobie. A striking example are the Enterprise Trusts, specifically concerned with promoting industry, business and employment in the community. In Glasgow, with a high rate of unemployment, the Clyde Workshops Ltd. was founded.

Clyde Workshops Ltd. was set up in January 1979 as a subsidiary company of the British Steel Corporation to provide and manage workshops and offices let at commercial rents to small firms. A back-up management advisory service is provided free to the tenants. It was set up by the B.S.C. to create viable employment in an area suffering from high unemployment as a result of steel plant closures. After a few years, the company intends to hive it off as an independent venture. It already operates without subsidies.

The response to the scheme has been rapid and very enthusiastic. Within nine months of opening, the available accommodation was fully let to sixty -five companies (fifty-three of which were first-time enterprises), employing over 500 people.

Enabling Development

The aim of institutes such as the Centre for Social Development at Emerson College, is to address the questions related to the development of individuals and organisations.[6] Many of the ideas described in this book have been developed in this way.

A way of describing their work is expressed as follows:

> 'Healing forces do not come out of abstract concepts and clever techniques, but from the ability of people to live into a social situation with understanding, warmth of heart, and a will to do what is needed. Therefore forces must be awakened

in the human being that recognise the relationship
between inner development and social responsibility.'

Also the new financial institutions, like Mercury Provident
Society Ltd., described in Chapter Four, and their associates
in Germany, Holland, Austria, Switzerland, Belgium, U.S.A.,
Australia and New Zealand, are working with great energy on
new approaches to financial questions. They are helping
numerous initiatives and organisations to create alternatives
bringing about social renewal.

In the appendix, one can find the names and addresses of a
number of initiatives that have been establised in the last ten
years. These initiatives hold in common the goal of contributing to a life on earth that is a response to the true needs of
others. They seek to make a space in which the being living in
each of us can become visible. All are inspired by a search
towards a life that brings the material and the spiritual
together, as in the old saying: 'Spirit is never without matter,
matter never without spirit'.

It is our hope and strong conviction that more initiatives
will develop as people wake up to the values that will shape a
new social future.

References

Introduction

1. The N.P.I. or Nederlands Pedagogisch Institute, founded by Professor B.C.J. Lievegoed, carries out consultancy, training and research in the social field. The Centre for Social Development at Emerson College is closely related to the N.P.I. and other consultancies such as Transform.

Chapter One

1. URBED – Urban and Economic Development Ltd. – fosters amongst other activities the development of new business and community projects. (99 Southwark St., London SE1 O3F, England).

   Dr. R. Lessem, director of Business Development Programme of City University and author of *The Roots of Excellence*, Fontana, London, and *Enterprise Development*, Gower, London.

   Kevin Kingsland, Centre for Human Communication (19 Pearsons Park, Hull, Humberside).

2. John Naisbitt, *Megatrends*, Warner Books, New York 1984.

3. Mercury Provident Society. A new banking institution aiming to bring consciousness and social responsibility in the realm of money (see Chapter Five).

Chapter Two

1. The Triodos Bank is a 'sister' bank to the British Mercury Provident Society Ltd., which is described in Chapter Four.

   Alexander Bos's ideas are also described in Martin Large, *Social Ecology*, Hawthorn Press 1981, Pages 135 – 137.

Chapter Three

1. See Owen Barfield, *Saving the Appearances: A Study of Idolatry*, Harcourt Brace Jovanovich, pp 71 – 95.

2. The relation between initiatives and individual development is described in more detail in Chapter Seven.

3. R. Steiner's *Motto of the Social Ethic* given to Edith Maryon 1917, R. Steiner, *Verses and Meditations*, Rudolf Steiner Press, 1979, p.117.

4. See P. Berger and T. Luckman, *The Social Construction of Reality A Treatise in the Sociology of Knowledge*, Doubleday 1966.

5. See Zeylmans van Emmichoven, *The Anthroposophical Understanding of the Human Soul*, Anthroposophic Press, 1983, pp 1 – 45.

6. See C. G. Jung, *Memories, Dreams and Reflections*, Random House 1961. Also Jung *Modern Man in Search of a Soul*, Harcourt, Brace Jovanovich 1933.
   Also David Schultz *Psychology, Anthroposophy and Self-transformation*, Journal for Anthroposophy – Autumn 1985.

7. Skolnick Report – *Survival or Excellence – A Study of Instructional Assignment in Ontario Colleges of Applied Arts and Technology* – July 1985, Ministry of Education, Ontario.

8. See 'Peoples Express Grows Bigger Without Getting Fat', *Wall Street Journal*, January 7th 1985.

9. John Naisbitt, *Megatrends, Ten Directions Transforming our Lives*, Warner Books, 1982, pp 211 – 231, also Peters and Waterman, *In Search of Excellence*.

10. This project is described in Christopher Schaefer and Ulf Stahlke, 'Co-operative Leadership, Supervisory Training at Ford, Cologne', *Journal of European Industrial Training*, Vol. 5, No.6.

Chapter Four

1. See B. Lievegoed, *Toward the 21st Century, Doing the Good*, Steiner Book Centre, Toronto, 1972, pp 56 – 75, for a more complete description of different types of groups. See also M. Large, *Social Ecology*, Hawthorn Press, 1981, pp 42 – 58.

2. See M. Large, *Social Ecology*, Hawthorn Press, U.K. 1981, pp 42 – 58.

Chapter Six

1. See Kenneth Boulding, 'General Systems Theory: The Skeleton of Science' *Management Science*, Vol.2, No.3, 1952. Also Gernier, L.E.,

'Evolution and Revolution as Organisations Grow', *Harvard Business Review*, July – August 1972.

2. J. Westphal, 'Henry Ford, Objective Idealist', *The Golden Blade*, 31st Issue, 1979, R. Steiner Press, London. Also Henry Ford, *My Life and Work*, William Heinemann Ltd., London, 1923, p.23.

3. See B. Lievegoed, *The Developing Organisation*, pp 51 – 61, Tavistock Publications, 1973. Republished by Celestial Arts, 1979, California.

4. M. Large, *Social Ecology*, pp 71 – 74, Hawthorn Press, Stroud, 1981.

5. E. Lehrs, *Republican, Not Democratic*, occasional paper available from the Rudolf Steiner Schools Fellowship, c/o Emerson College, Forest Row, Sussex.

6. See B. Lievegoed, *The Developing Organisation*, pp 71 – 76. Also M. Large, *Social Ecology*.

7. See T. J. Peters and R. H. Waterman, Jr., *In Search of Excellence: Lessons from America's Best Run Companies*, Warner Books Edition, 1982, pp 29 – 55.
    Also J. Naisbitt, *Megatrends*, Warner Books, 1982, pp 103 – 140, 211 – 231.

8. Peters and Waterman, Op. Cit.

9. Ibid., pp 89 – 306.

10. See *The Phases of Organisation Development*, occasional paper, NPI Institute for Organisation Development, Zeist, Holland.

11. See R. Steiner, *Theosophy*, Anthroposophic Press, Spring Valley, N.Y., 1971, pp 1 – 39.

12. See Robert Chin, 'The Utility of Systems Models and Developmental Models for Practitioners', in Bennis, Benne and Chin, *The Planning of Change* (New York: Holt, Rinehart and Winston. 1962). pp 201 – 215.

13. Servant Leader Institute, Townsend and Bottum Case Study, June 1985, Ann Arber, M.I.48069, Section 5 – Building an Ethical Business Climate.

Chapter Seven

1. See Rudolf Steiner, *Occult Science*, Anthroposophic Press, 1972. Also Paul Eugen Schiller, *Rudolf Steiner and Initiation*, Anthroposophic Press,

1981, pp 31 – 36.

2. See R. Steiner, *Knowledge of the Higher Worlds and Its Attainment,* Anthroposophic Press, 1983, p.19.

3. See R. Steiner, 'How Can the Psychological Distress of Today be Overcome', in *Some Results of Spiritual Investigation,* Steiner Books, pp 105 – 106, New York, for a penetrating description of these difficulties.

4. Marjorie Spock, *Reflections on Community Building.* Self-published. This excellent essay contains many important insights on human relationships. Available through St. George Books, Spring Valley, New York 10977.

5. See *Journal for Anthroposophy,* Number 37, Summer, 1983

6. See Chapter Five.

7. B. Lievegoed, *Toward the 21st Century, Doing the Good,* Rudolf Steiner Publications, Toronto, 1983.

8. See Paul Eugen Schiller, *Rudolf Steiner and Initiation,* Anthroposophic Press, Spring Valley, N.Y., 1981, for an account of the meditative disciplines connected to Anthroposophy, a philosophical orientation on which much of the content of this book is based.

Chapter Eight

1. Life and Work-Community, Arta, Krakelingweg 25, 3707 EP Zeist, Holland.

2. B.C.J. Lievegoed, *Phases,* Rudolf Steiner Press, London.

3. B.C.J. Lievegoed, *Man on the Threshold,* Hawthorn Press, Stroud, U.K., 1984.

4. Gudrun Davy & Bons Voors, *Lifeways,* Hawthorn Press, Stroud, U.K., 1983.

5. Forum 3, Gymnasiumstrasse 21, D-7000 Stuttgart 1, West Germany.

6. N.P.I. The Centre for Social Development and Transform Ltd. are both daughter institutes of the N.P.I. (Nederlands Pedagogisch Institute) a leading Dutch consultancy addressing individual and organisational questions in business, education and government. There are linked institutes in Scandinavia, Australia, New Zealand, U.S.A., Germany and South Africa.

Appendix

The Social Ecology Series

Vision in Action is the fourth book in the Social Ecology Series. Vision follows *Social Ecology – Exploring Post-Industrial Society; Man on the Threshold – the Challenge of Inner Development* by Bernard Lievegoed; *Hope, Evolution and Change* by John Davy.

The series aims to address current social, human, ecological and spiritual questions. A basic value is that in order to work with these questions constructively, inner development needs to accompany outer action. The books arise from the work of different groups and networks of people – when their work has reached a certain maturity, of use to a wider audience. Each book is therefore both a working and a study book.

By social ecology – literally 'social house wisdom' – is meant both the understanding of the processes of development in the natural, social and human spheres, and the fostering of such development. Just as living organisms and their environments are interdependant – so too are individuals, groups and organisations.

Forthcoming books in the Autumn and Winter 1986 in the Social Ecology Series are:

Dying Forests – A Crisis in Consciousness by Jochen Bockemühl (August 1986);

Ariadne's Awakening by Betty Staley, Margli Matthews and Signe Schaefer;

Introducing Rudolf Steiner by Rudi Lissau, a book on new ways of handling *Money*, and a book on drugs.

Judy and Martin Large: June 1986.

Orders: The above books are available from Hawthorn Press, The Mount, Main Road, Whiteshill, Stroud, GL6 6JA. Stroud (04536) 77040.

About the Authors

Christopher Schaefer Ph.D., is a founding member of Social Ecology Associates and a co-founder of the Centre for Social Development at Emerson College in England. He has worked in the fields of organisation and community development for ten years. During this time he has worked with a variety of clients in England, Germany and the United States, including Kimberton Farms School, Ford Motor Company, Seneca College, Lamb Studios and many other initiatives. Prior to his work with Social Ecology Associates he taught Social Science at the Massachusetts Institute of Technology. He is currently a faculty member of the Waldorf Institute in Spring Valley, New York.

Tijno Voors, lecturer at the Centre for Social Development, Emerson College in England, works as a consultant on questions of community and organisation development. He has been closely involved with Mercury Provident Society Ltd. in England and Triodos NV in Holland – two new banking initiatives on approaches to handling money. He worked for many years as a management consultant with the N.P.I. Institute for Organisation Development in Holland and Social Ecology Associates in England. He lives with his wife and three children in Sussex, England.

Warren Ashe is a founder director (1974) of Mercury Provident Society and is an active board member. He is particularly interested in the problems of associations, policies and incomes. Born in New York in 1935, he came to England at the age of sixteen and has had a long career in teaching and school administration on the financial side. He teaches humanities subjects in Michael Hall School, Sussex.

Stephen Briault MA was born in England and educated in London and Cambridge. He worked for several years in therapeutic communities and later in educational administration and finance. After a period of involvement in refugee resettlements, he trained at the Centre for Social Development where he is now a member of the teaching staff. He is also active as trainer and consultant for diverse organisations, and in career counselling.

Contacts List of Initiatives

1. Banking Initiatives

Many people who make bank deposits feel dissatisfied at knowing little of how these investment monies are used. It is not possible for them to be involved in the bank's investment decisions. New Banking Institutions are founded to encourage depositors to influence the way in which their deposits are applied. They seek to bring the depositor and borrower together, so that each is aware of the other's intentions and purposes. In practical terms, this means that the project which needs money is described so that the depositor can recognise the nature of the impulse behind the project.

The task of these banks often includes business counselling, as people setting out on new ventures need sound advice in handling assets and money. Ordinary business criteria are brought to bear to judge the project, as well as criteria related to the impulse, to sense whether the initiative responds to an urgent need, adopts a strong and healthy social form and will contribute to social renewal in the widest sense.

The Mercury Provident Society Ltd.
Orlingbury House
Lewes Road
Forest Row
East Sussex RH18 5AA
England

Triodosbank NV
Stationslaan 4
Postbus 55
3700 AB Zeist
Holland

GLS Gemeinschaftsbank eG
Oskar-Hoffman Strasse 25
4630 Bochum
West Germany

Rudolf Steiner Foundation
RDI
Box 147a
Chatham
N.Y. 12037
U.S.A.

Southern Cross Capital Exchange
38 Lawton View Road
Wentworth Falls
N.S.W. 2782
Australia

Prometheus Foundation
P.O. Box 1397
Hastings
New Zealand

2. *Centre for Social Development (Emerson College)*

The Centre for Social Development at Emerson College offers a practical and basic foundation in questions of social life. They are intended for people working directly with social issues and for those who wish to add a more conscious dimension to their work. Participants can come for a year's course, and intensive 12 week term, course of one/two or three weeks or weekend workships. People who have completed the first year are offered a second year of professionalisation in the field of adult education and consultancy.

Courses are designed to provide a schooling in questions of social life out of the perspective of Anthroposophy. They exist for people working directly with social issues, and for those who wish to add a more conscious social dimension to their work. Participants come from many different countries, creating a truly international atmosphere, and range in age from the early twenties into the sixties.

Related to the Centre for Social Development are a number of consultancy groups, who aim to help individuals, groups and organisations to take a next step in their development:

Centre for Social Development
Old Plaw Hatch House
Sharpthorne
West Sussex RH19 4JL
England

Social Ecology Associates
23 Raymond Avenue
Spring Valley
New York 10977
U.S.A.

Transform
Silver Birches, Edge
Stroud
Gloucestershire
England

Social Ecology Associates
Willunga Crescent
Forestville
N.S.W. 2087
Australia

Social Ekology Associates
Kärralundsgatan 55
S-41656 Göteborg
Sweden

Social Ecology Associates
37 Summer Street
Ponsonby
Aukland 1
New Zealand

N.P.I., Institute for Organisation Development
Valckenboschlaan 8
3707 CR Zeist
Holland

B.G.O., Beraterverband für Gegenwartsfragen und Organisationsent-
wickelung
Nägelseestrasse 23
7800 Freiburg
West Germany

N.P.I., Instituto de Desenvolvimento Organizacional SC
Rua Lacedemonia 239
04634 Sao Paulo
Brasil

Odisa, Organisation Development Institute of Southern Africa
P.O. Box 92176
Norwood 2117
South Africa

3. Drug Rehabilitation Centres

Drug Rehabilitation Centres, like ARTA in Holland, offer a therapeutic
community to people who want to overcome their problems with drug
addiction. The purpose of the programme is to bring healing to the
disturbances in normal development, and open ways to find one's
individual life aims and direction. People stay for an average of one year
to eighteen months in the living and work-community.

ARTA, Life and Work-Community
Krakelingweg 25
3707 HP Zeist
Holland

Melchiors Grund
D623 Schwalm Tal
Hopfgarten
West Germany

Die Sieben Zwergen
Detlef Kratschmann
D-7777 Salem
Germany

4. Life Centres

Life Centres, like Forum 3 in Stuttgart, West Germany, have created a 'Teestube' (tea house) for young people. It has a bookshop, a theatre, and offers many educational activities and cultural events. Its main purpose is to create a space where people can meet. Out of this meeting people get to know each other, find courage to take a course or find a group that wants to take an initiative. The meeting is the bridge to a new future for many of the people who come to this place.

People are able to make music, play games, read, follow courses, get information, etc. Simple snacks and drinks are offered. The spaces are simple, have warm colours and furniture.

About 4,000 young people between 18 and 30 visit Forum 3 every month.

Forum 3
Gymnasiumstrasse 21
Stuttgart
West Germany

Helios Fountain
Grassmarket 7
Edinburgh EH12 HY
Scotland

Shire Training Workshops
The British School
Slad Road
Stroud GL5 1QW
England

The Institute for Social Development
P.O. Box 350
Roseville
N.S.W.2069
Australia

Rudolf Steiner Centre Toronto
P.O. Box 472, Station Z
Toronto
Ontario M5N 2Z6
Canada

Social Development Initiative West
1540 Scenic Avenue
Berkeley CA 94700
U.S.A.

5. *Rudolf Steiner/Waldorf Schools*

The Waldorf movement recognises that schools should be truly comprehensive: open to all girls and boys aged 4 to 18 of normal capability; with a curriculum for all pupils which is as broad as time will allow; and with a healthy balance of artistic and practical, alongside academic activities. Waldorf schools, each in its own way, set out to meet these objectives.

Teachers in Waldorf schools are dedicated to generating a genuine inner enthusiasm for learning within every child.

One of the most notable ways in which the Waldorf approach to education differs from others is in the response of the curriculum to the various phases of child development; another, related to this, is the crucial though changing relationship between teacher and child as these various phases are met.

Contact can be made with:

Steiner Schools Fellowship
Orlingbury House
Lewes Road
Forest Row
East Sussex
RH18 5AA
England

Association of Waldorf Schools of North America
Cambridge Avenue
Garden City
N.Y. 11530
U.S.A.

Association of Rudolf Steiner Schools in Australia
P.O. Box 82
Round Corner
Dural 2158
Australia

Social Ecology Series: In Print

SOCIAL ECOLOGY
Exploring Post Industrial Society

Martin Large

Social Ecology looks at the development of individuals, groups, organisations and society in the post-industrial age.

Pb; 210 x 145mm, 162pp;
ISBN 950 706 221
£3.95 or US$7.95
1983

MAN ON THE THRESHOLD
The Challenge of Inner Development

Bernard Lievegoed M.D.

The author of **Phases,** and the **Developing Organisations** describes the challenge of inner development today. Eastern and western meditative paths are described, and there are sections on personal development and counselling.

Pb. full colour cover;
210 x 135mm;
224pp; £7.95 or US$12.95
ISBN 0950 706 26 4
1985

DYING FORESTS
A Crisis in Consciousness
Transforming our way of life.

46 colour pictures and text by Jochen Bockemühl.
Introduction by Professor Brian Goodwin.
Translated by John Meeks.

Forests are dying in central Europe – many trees are dying in the Swiss mountains, threatening erosion problems. Many lakes in Scandinavia, Scotland and North Wales now have no fish. Sulphur dioxide, ozone, nitric oxides from industry, traffic and power stations are some causes. But what part do people play in causing forest die-back?

Dying Forests offers the insights of Jochen Bockemühl – both scientist and artist – into the underlying causes of forest die-back.

The author, by means of his water colour sketches and commentary, describes how, through the development of a sensitive observation of landscape ecology, a more conscious encounter with nature can take place. Through the exercises described in **Dying Forests,** the strength to change one's habits and our destructive technology may emerge. **Dying Forests** is a striking example of the use of Goethe's scientific method which aims to understand the living whole, rather than the dead parts.

Jochen Bockemühl is a scientist working at the Goetheanum Research Laboratory in Dornach, Switzerland. He has lectured and conducted many 'observation workshops' in the English speaking world. His work on plant metamorphosis is included in Open University biology course texts.

Sewn limp bound; full colour cover;
210 x 210mm, 96pp;
46 water colour illustrations in full colour, plus drawings;
£8.95 or US$15.00;
ISBN 1 869 890 02 7
1986

ARIADNE'S AWAKENING

Taking up the threads of consciousness.

Margli Matthews,
Signe Schaefer
and Betty Staley

Much has been written about women and men in terms of rôles, gender and social forms through the ages. The past two decades have witnessed widespread change in 'rights' and 'equality' on external levels, but this has not always made for more human fulfillment. The authors acknowledge the context of feminism, but broaden its picture enormously. They view 'masculine' and 'feminine' not just as bodily forms, but as principles of meaning: principles at work within each of us, in society and indeed in the entire span of Earth evolution.

Ariadne's Awakening traces through myth and history the journey humankind has made up to the present; it considers phases of life, relationships for men and women, and confronts such issues as the scientific management of conception and death, the rape of Earth's natural resources and the need for a New Feminine to influence values and decisions for the future.

Ariadne's Awakening is a book about understanding ourselves, and a search for a creative balance.

Signe Schaefer teaches at the Waldorf Institute, Spring Valley, New York. Margli Matthews teaches at Emerson College, Sussex and Betty Staley teaches in California. Signe and Margli were founder members of the Ariadne Women's Group, and wrote articles for **Lifeways.**

Sewn limp bound;
210 x 135mm, 220pp approx;
£6.95 or US$12.95;
ISBN 1 869 890 01 9
1986
To be published in German.

HOPE, EVOLUTION AND CHANGE

John Davy.
Introduction by
Owen Barfield

The twenty-seven articles in this book reflect the author's work as a scientist, journalist and lecturer: articles on evolutionary questions, language, education, science, caring for the planet, life after life and contemporary thinkers like Schumacher and Elizabeth Kübler-Ross.

Colin Wilson '. . . a significant figure . . .' review of **Hope** in **Resurgence.**

Paperback; 210 x 135mm; 274pp; £5.95 or US$9.95; ISBN 0 950 706 27 2 1985
To be published in German.

Social Ecology Series: Books in Preparation for 1987

RUDOLF STEINER
An Introduction

Rudi Lissau

This book gives a vivid picture of Rudolf Steiner's life and work. It aims to point out the relevance of Steiner's activities to contemporary social and human concerns.
There are chapters on Steiner's philosophy; his view of the universe, earth and the human being; Christ and human destiny; the meditative path; education and social development; approaches to Rudolf Steiner's work and obstacles.

Rudi Lissau has taught adolescents at Wynstones School for over forty years. He has written and lectured widely in North America, the UK, Scandinavia and Central Europe.

Sewn limp bound; 210 x 135mm; 192pp approx; ISBN 1 869 890 06 X 1987

DRUGS – THE WORK OF ARTA

Drugs (provisional title) addresses the problems of hard drug taking, and the insights gained by the co-workers of ARTA in Holland in assisting drug addicts.

MONEY, SOUL AND SPIRIT

Glen Saunders and Stephen Briault

Money is based on the authors' experience and insights gained through working with money in 'conventional' and 'alternative' settings, including the provision of community banking and advisory services to a wide range of individuals and organisations. Was D.H. Lawrence right when he wrote that money 'poisons you when you've got it and starves you when you haven't'? How can we take hold of it in ways which support our bodily existence without enslaving our hearts and minds? How must we change our thinking, feeling and doing so that money can find its healthy place within the human community? The book does not offer tax advice, or tell you how to get rich: it takes its starting point from the fundamental questions people face today with the tremendous broadening of inner and outer choices. New spiritual directions, changing values in relationships, new attitudes to work and to working with others, a stronger sense of individual biography and personal development – all these indicate the context and the need for a change in our perspectives and approaches to money. This will be taken up for organisations, initiative groups and personal life. Some of the themes covered will be:

– managing and metamorphosing money
– possession: needs and wants
– humanising money: overcoming hypnosis and fear
– ensouling investment: savings and lending
– transforming work and payment
– welfare, charity, productivity
– inheritance and dependence

Stephen Briault works at the Centre for Social Development at Emerson College. Glen Saunders is an accountant and works for Mercury Provident plc.

Publication: Summer/Autumn 1987

Who's Bringing Them Up? Series

FESTIVALS, FAMILY AND FOOD

Diana Carey and Judy Large

'Packed full of ideas on things to do, food to make, songs to sing and games to play, it's an invaluable resources book designed to help you and your family celebrate the various festival days scattered round the year.'

The Observer

Paperback; full colour cover;
250 x 200mm; 216pp;
over 200 illustrations; £6.95 or
US$12.95;
ISBN 0 950 706 23 X
Fourth Impression.

LIFEWAYS
Working with family questions

Gudrun Davy
and Bons Voors

Lifeways is about children, about family life, about being a parent. But most of all it is about freedom, and how the tension between family life and personal fulfillment can be resolved.

'These essays affirm that creating a family, even if you are a father on your own, or a working mother, can be a joyful, positive and spiritual work. The first essay is one of the wisest and balanced discussions of women's rôles I have read.'

Fiona Handley,
Church of England Newspaper

Paperback; colour cover;
150 x 210mm; 316pp;
£5.95 or US$11.95;
ISBN 0 950 706 24 8
Third impression 1985;
Lifeways is published in German and Dutch.

THE CHILDREN'S YEAR
Crafts and clothes for children to make

Stephanie Cooper,
Christine Fynes-Clinton,
Marija Rowling

Here is a book which hopes to give the possibility to adults and children alike to rediscover the joy and satisfaction of making something that they know looks and feels good and which can also be played with imaginatively. It takes us through Spring, Summer, Autumn and Winter with appropriate gifts and toys to create, including full, clear instructions and illustrations. There is children's clothing as well, particularly meant to be made of natural fabrics to let the child's body breathe while growing. There are soft items for play and beauty, and there are firm solid wooden ones; moving toys such as balancing birds or climbing gnomes; horses which move when you add children to them! From woolly hats to play houses, mobiles or dolls, here are 112 potential treasures to make in seasonal groupings.

Hard back; full colour cover;
267 x 216mm;
220pp; several hundred illustrations;
£9.95 or US $15.00
ISBN 1 869 890 00 0
1986

Books in Preparation

THE INCARNATING CHILD

Joan Salter

Even in to-day's modern scientific world, the mystery and miracle of conception, pregnancy and birth stir within many people a sense of wonder. **The Incarnating Child** picks up Wordsworth's theme – 'our Birth is but a sleep and a forgetting . . .' and follows the Soul life of tiny babies well into childhood. It is full of practical advice for mothers, fathers, relations or anyone concerned with childcare. Joan Salter examines pregnancy, birth, early infancy, babyhood, childhood on up to adolescence. She addresses physical development, the formation of healthy personalities, nutrition, clothing, environment, toys and learning, immunization and health, and the acquisition of skills and thinking ability. She writes with an astounding attention to detail, and the voice of years of experience in her field. Joan Salter is a specialist in maternal and child care, and has nursing background which included work with migrant workers and displaced persons. She is the founder and director of the Gabriel Baby Centre, since 1976 a centre for maternal and child welfare in Melbourne, and is essentially concerned with the upbringing of the child in the home.

Full colour cover; 210 x 135mm; 220pp approx; illustrations and photos; ISBN 1 869 890 3 1987

FOODWAYS

Wendy Cook

Foodways follows up Wendy Cook's article in **Lifeways.** Various questions are covered such as nutrition and medicine, vegetarian and animal foods, quality in food, therapeutic views of food, food and child development, social and community aspects of mealtimes, guidelines for food preparation, and some of the author's tried and tasted recipes. Wendy Cook teaches home economics, advises on nutritional questions, has cooked at Emerson college and has studied nutritional questions extensively.

Publication in Autumn 1987